GOSPEL FOUNDATIONS

The God Who Creates

VOL. 1	GENESIS

LifeWay Press® • Nashville, Tennessee

From the creators of *The Gospel Project*, Gospel Foundations is a six-volume
resource that teaches the storyline of Scripture. It is comprehensive in scope
yet concise enough to be completed in just one year. Each seven-session
volume includes videos to help your group understand the way each text
fits into the storyline of the Bible.

© 2018 LifeWay Press®

ISBN 978-1-5359-0358-5 • Item 005803632

Dewey decimal classification: 230
Subject headings: CHRISTIANITY / GOSPEL / SALVATION

EDITORIAL TEAM

Michael Kelley
Director, Groups Ministry

Brian Dembowczyk
Managing Editor

Joel Polk
Editorial Team Leader

Daniel Davis, Josh Hayes
Content Editors

Brian Daniel
Manager, Short-Term Discipleship

Darin Clark
Art Director

We believe that the Bible has God for its author; salvation for its end; and
truth, without any mixture of error, for its matter and that all Scripture
is totally true and trustworthy. To review LifeWay's doctrinal guideline,
please visit lifeway.com/doctrinalguideline.

To order additional copies of this resource, write to LifeWay Resources Customer
Service; One LifeWay Plaza; Nashville, TN 37234; fax 615-251-5933; call toll
free 800-458-2772; order online at LifeWay.com; email orderentry@lifeway.com;
or visit the LifeWay Christian Store serving you.

Printed in the United States of America

Groups Ministry Publishing
LifeWay Resources
One LifeWay Plaza
Nashville, TN 37234

Contents

About *The Gospel Project*

Gospel Foundations is from the creators of *The Gospel Project*, which exists to point kids, students, and adults to the gospel of Jesus Christ through weekly group Bible studies and additional resources that show how God's plan of redemption unfolds throughout Scripture and still today, compelling them to join the mission of God.

The Gospel Project provides theological yet practical, age-appropriate Bible studies that immerse your entire church in the story of the gospel, helping to develop a gospel culture that leads to gospel mission.

Gospel Story

Immersing people of all ages in the storyline of Scripture: God's plan to rescue and redeem His creation through His Son, Jesus Christ.

Gospel Culture

Inspiring communities where the gospel saturates our experience and doubters become believers who become declarers of the gospel.

Gospel Mission

Empowering believers to live on mission, declaring the good news of the gospel in word and deed.

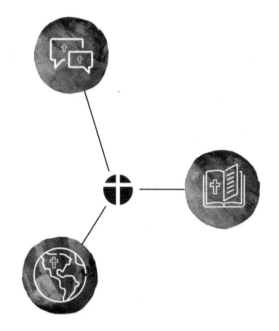

How to Use This Study

This Bible-study book includes seven weeks of content for group and personal study.

Group Study

Regardless of what day of the week your group meets, each week of content begins with the group session. Each group session uses the following format to facilitate simple yet meaningful interaction among group members and with God's Word.

Introducing the Study & Setting the Context
These pages include **content and questions** to get the conversation started and **infographics** to help group members see the flow of the biblical storyline.

Continuing the Discussion
Each session has a corresponding **teaching video** to help tell the Bible story. These videos have been created specifically to challenge the group to consider the entire story of the Bible. After watching the video, continue the **group discussion** by reading the Scripture passages and discussing the questions on these pages. Finally, conclude each group session with **a personal missional response** based on what God has said through His Word.

Personal Study

Three personal studies are provided for each session to take individuals deeper into Scripture and to supplement the content introduced in the group study. With **biblical teaching and introspective questions**, these sections challenge individuals to grow in their understanding of God's Word and to respond in faith.

Leader Guide

A tear-out leader guide for each session is provided on pages 95-108, which includes possible answers to questions highlighted with an icon and suggestions for various sections of the group study.

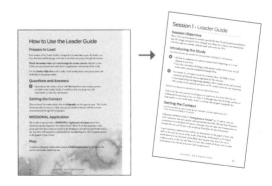

God's Word to You

A Summary of the Bible

In the beginning, the all-powerful, personal God created the universe. This God created human beings in His image to live joyfully in His presence, in humble submission to His gracious authority. But all of us have rebelled against God and, in consequence, must suffer the punishment of our rebellion: physical death and the wrath of God.

Thankfully, God initiated a rescue plan, which began with His choosing the nation of Israel to display His glory in a fallen world. The Bible describes how God acted mightily on Israel's behalf, rescuing His people from slavery and then giving them His holy law. But God's people—like all of us—failed to rightly reflect the glory of God.

Then, in the fullness of time, in the person of Jesus Christ, God Himself came to renew the world and to restore His people. Jesus perfectly obeyed the law given to Israel. Though innocent, He suffered the consequences of human rebellion by His death on a cross. But three days later, God raised Him from the dead.

Now the church of Jesus Christ has been commissioned by God to take the news of Christ's work to the world. Empowered by God's Spirit, the church calls all people everywhere to repent of sin and to trust in Christ alone for our forgiveness. By God's grace in Christ, repentance and faith restores our relationship with God and results in a life of ongoing transformation.

The Bible promises that Jesus Christ will return to this earth as the conquering King. Only those who live in repentant faith in Christ will escape God's judgment and live joyfully in God's presence for all eternity. God's message is the same to all of us: repent and believe, before it is too late. Confess with your mouth that Jesus is Lord and believe with your heart that God raised Him from the dead, and you will be saved.

God Creates

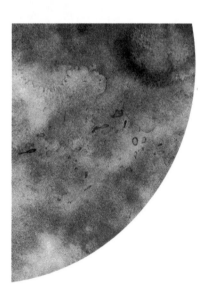

Introducing the Study

In the beginning...

These three words serve as a launching pad. They set the stage for the story of everything that comes next. They serve as the foundation for all we know, experience, love, and understand. And yet, these three words lose their meaning without the next word we find in Scripture:

In the beginning, *God*...

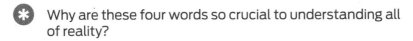 Why are these four words so crucial to understanding all of reality?

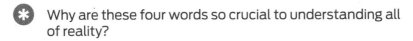 What do these words teach us about the nature of God?

Setting the Context

God was there at the beginning of the storyline of Scripture—and so was the Son of God, which the New Testament makes explicit: The Son is before all things and He created all things (Col. 1:16-17). **"Seeing Jesus in Genesis"** (p. 11) shows just some of the ways the centrality of Jesus in Scripture was the plan of God from the very beginning.

> How can Christ connections throughout Scripture help us make sense of God's Word?

Also vital to the beginning of Scripture is **the doctrine of creation *ex nihilo*,** a Latin phrase that means "out of nothing."

We use the word *create* when we cause something to come into being, but we always form something out of other things that previously existed. We create music using notes, art out of paints and a canvas, books from words, language, paper, and binding.

God, however, created from nothing. Everything in existence came to be because of Him—rocks, trees, the very air we breathe. Not only that, but intangible realities such as courage, love, and laughter come from Him as well. All of this came from the heart of God at the beginning.

So this is where our story begins—with nothing. Nothing except God, and then came much, much more.

> What are some of the ways we might, through our lives, neglect the fact that God is our Creator?

✝ CHRIST Connection

Jesus is the perfect image of the invisible God, the only One who rules wisely over creation, perfectly relates to God and others, and through His work, earns our everlasting rest. By the Son, for the Son, and through the Son, all things exist and hold together.

Seeing **Jesus** *in* **Genesis**

Old Testament	New Testament
The First Adam Brought Death (Gen. 3)	**The Second Adam** Brought Life (Rom. 5)
The Protoevangelium The Promise of Deliverance from the Serpent (Gen. 3:15)	**The Fulfillment** Jesus Destroys the Works of the Devil (1 John 3:8)
Abel's Blood Cries Out for Justice (Gen. 4)	**Jesus' Blood** Proclaims Forgiveness (Heb. 12:24)
The Almost Sacrifice of Isaac "The LORD Will Provide" (Gen. 22)	**The Crucifixion of Jesus** "The Lamb of God" (John 1:29)
Joseph Suffered According to God's Plan (Gen. 50:20)	**Jesus Suffered** According to God's Plan (Acts 2:23)

Continuing the Discussion

 Watch this session's video, and then continue the group discussion using the following guide.

What ideas or phrases regarding God as Creator were most striking to you in the video? Why?

In what ways is this biblical truth—human beings are the pinnacle of God's creation—affirmed in our culture? Denied in our culture?

As a group, read Genesis 1:1-2,31.

 What are some of the things we can learn about the nature and character of God from these verses alone?

Why might spending time in God's creation be a valuable exercise for the Christian?

Why is it important for us to remember not only that God created everything but that He created everything good?

How might our lives go off track if we fail to recognize this truth?

God is not only our Creator, He is also our good Creator. When we embrace God as our Creator, we must also embrace the truth that we owe Him our obedience. If we fail to see creation as God's activity, then we can and will easily justify any kind of disobedience.

As a group, read Genesis 1:26-28; 2:16-25.

What is different about the way God created humans from everything else?

What do you think it means to be created in God's image?

✱ Why is it important that we recognize that all humans are created in God's image?

To be created in God's image means that we have a unique ability to relate intimately with God and others. When we recognize this fact, we can only conclude that every human being is deserving of respect and honor.

As a group, read Colossians 1:15-17.

What description of Jesus sticks out to you the most in these verses?

What do these verses tell us about the process and purpose of creation?

✱ How does it change our perspective of creation and life to recognize that all things were created by the Son, through the Son, and for the Son?

The Bible is a God-centered book. We have been given Scripture so that we might know God. That means when we read Scripture, we should focus primarily on what we can learn, love, and embrace about God and His Son, Jesus.

✝ MISSIONAL Application

Record in this space at least one way you will apply the truth of Scripture as an image bearer of God.

Personal Study 1

God creates everything good.

Read Genesis 1:1-2,31.

How else could you describe the creation of everything unless you're first introduced to the Someone who preceded everything? That's the whole point of Genesis 1:1. The God who simply is, who preceded everything and is not dependent on anything, created all that we know and all that we don't know as well.

The original audience of the Book of Genesis was the ancient Israelites on their way to the promised land (a story for a later time). They likely would not have been asking some of the questions that pique our interest, such as the age of the earth or the science behind creation. So what, then, was the original purpose for the creation account in Genesis?

The Israelites would have wrestled with questions such as these: "Is our God the real God?"; "Is He the best God?"; and "Is He the most powerful God?" Having lived so long among the gods of the Egyptians and being introduced to the gods of the foreign nations that surrounded them, the Israelites struggled to believe that their God was *the* God.

To remedy such wandering hearts, God wrote Genesis 1:1 to help His people understand that the God of their bedtime stories—the God of their fathers and their fathers' fathers—was the very same God who created the world.

We are no different than the original audience of the Book of Genesis. Though perhaps not tempted to bow down to wooden statues, our hearts are just as prone to wander. Lazy Sundays instead of early Sunday worship sure sound nice. You dream about all the things you could've bought with the money you gave the church by the end of the year. There's an ever-present guilt each time your eyes steal a glimpse of your attractive coworker.

Obedience, at times, seems too costly, and our hearts wonder: *Is God real? Does He love me? Is He worth it?* When we have these questions and struggle to believe in the realness and goodness of God, He wants us to recount Genesis 1:1: "In the beginning, God..." When there was nothing but nothing, God was, and that ought to create in us a sense of wonder about Him that trumps all our other wonderings.

But not only did God create everything, God created everything good. When God created something and called it good, He was saying it was doing well at performing its intended purpose and design.

So what is the purpose and design of creation? To declare God's glory and proclaim the work of His hands (Ps. 19:1). To reveal things about God that are invisible to us (Rom. 1:20). Creation reveals God's eternal power and divine nature in a way that we should clearly see and understand them. The purpose and design of creation is to tell of the glory of God, to display plainly His power and His divine nature. When God created the heavens, the stars, the trees, the mountains, the birds, and the animals, they did their job well, and God called them good. They're still doing their job well, even if it is now obscured as a result of sin in the world.

How does creation still testify about the nature and character of God?

How should the reality that God is the Creator of everything and that He created everything good impact the way you live each day?

Personal Study 2

God creates people in His image.

Read Genesis 1:26-28; 2:16-25.

God created, and God created everything good. In the first three days of creation, God dealt with its formlessness by giving boundaries—separating and organizing to make the heavens, the seas, and the land. Then, in the second set of three days, God dealt with the emptiness of the world by filling the spheres that He had created in the first three days. He filled the expanse with the sun, moon, and stars, and He filled the sky, seas, and land with living creatures. Throughout all of this, God stepped back from each moment in creation and "saw that it was good." But the crown jewel of His creation was still to come. God created humankind in a unique way from everything else in the universe.

In this aspect of creation, we see God not just displaying His power by commanding, "Let there be human beings," as He did with all the other elements of creation, but He also displayed His closeness toward humanity in fashioning the first people. He began by forming Adam from the dirt, shaping him, and breathing life into his nostrils.

The key here is to notice that God created man in His own image (Gen. 1:26). To bear God's image fully means to have a relationship with Him. We were not merely spoken into existence by God's power but formed by His hands to hold His very breath. We were created not just by power but through intimacy—for the purpose of relationship.

Our image-bearing relationship started when God created us. The account in Genesis 2 shows how powerful a scene this was, when God's face was toward us, when He breathed into the first man the breath of life. Just as a mirror best reflects an image when the mirror is in perfect "relationship" with, or directly in front of, the object that it's imaging, so too do we best reflect God's image when we are rightly aligned with Him in relationship. We reflect God best—we image Him best—in two ways: in our relationships and in our stewardship.

Being made in God's image means we are meant to be relational creatures. In other words, we are best able to show the world who our God is and what He is like when we walk closely with Him, meeting with Him daily through His Word and prayer. God's desire is that we live in intimacy with Him, for we alone among creation have the capacity to do so since we are created in God's image.

But bearing God's image doesn't point only to the relationship we have with God; we also have relationships with each other. God created us "male and female." The triune God who exists in communion by nature—Father, Son, and Holy Spirit—created human beings to live in communion with one another as well.

After multiple statements of God seeing His creation and saying it was "good," then came the first moment when something was described as "not good"—the man whom God had formed was alone. We were not created to bear God's image on our own, to have an isolated relationship with God. We reflect God best when we are in community with one another, relating to others in the love and grace of God, and when we are pursuing an intimate relationship with Him ourselves. This is the core of what it means to be made in God's image.

Not only do we image God in our relational capacity, we also image Him in our stewardship. When God placed humankind in the garden, He immediately gave these humans work to do. They were to care for and cultivate the garden as His representatives in worship of Him. As they worked and rested and cared for the earth, they were to do so in the same way God cares for all of creation. Because we are created in God's image, we are to mirror that image in the way we steward everything God has given us charge over.

Because we are image bearers of God, we reflect His glory in how we steward the earth, work and rest, and cultivate relationships with Him and others.

What does the fact that all people are created in God's image indicate about the way every human being should be treated?

What are some of the barriers in your own life to living in true community?

Personal Study 3

God creates everything through the Son and for the Son.

Read Colossians 1:15-17.

Why did God create? Was it because He was lonely? Because there was something deficient in Himself? To fulfill some need that He had? Far from any of these reasons. God created not because He was lacking but because He was overflowing—spilling over with the perfect fellowship between the three Persons of the Trinity from the very beginning.

It's not uncommon for people to misunderstand the nature of the Trinity—one God in three Persons—to mean that at creation, God was the Father, then in Bethlehem, God became the Son, and then in the Book of Acts, God became the Holy Spirit. This is not true and is actually an ancient heresy called modalism. Contrary to this, the Bible teaches that God has always and eternally existed in these three distinct Persons of Father, Son, and Holy Spirit. Even more, the Bible teaches us that God created everything through the Son and for the Son.

These New Testament verses from the Book of Colossians work in concert with the account of creation from Genesis to show us this truth. This passage of Scripture teaches that Christ was "before all things," which indicates that He is eternal. Christ is not created; He is the eternal Creator. Whenever the beginning took place, He was already there making everything become a reality. In John 8:58, while debating with the Jewish leaders, Jesus made it clear that He was preexistent and divine: "Before Abraham was, I am."

Christ not only created all things but He also maintains the entire cosmos. He sustains the order in the universe. He holds it all together. Doesn't this give you hope? If He holds the universe together, surely He can hold our lives together as Christians! Whenever we are tempted to give up hope, to feel like we can barely "hold it together," like the world is spinning out of control, we ought to remember that God is God and we are not. Jesus holds everything together by the power of who He is!

Jesus is the perfect image of the invisible God, the only One who rules wisely over creation, perfectly relates to God and others, and through His work, earns our everlasting rest. By the Son, for the Son, and through the Son, all things exist and hold together.

It is through Jesus that all things were created; it is through Jesus that all things hold together; and it is for the glory of Jesus that everything exists. The most basic implication this truth has for us is that we, like everything else in creation, exist through and for Jesus. It would be a drastic mistake for us, then, to read the story of the Bible as if we were the main character in Scripture. We are not. We are supporting players, and we only find true meaning and purpose when we align our lives with God for the glory of Jesus rather than trying to find how He fits into ours.

When we read the Bible, then, we should not be asking primarily how this passage or text relates to me and my story. Instead, we must read Scripture as the revelation of God that we might know Him and His Son. Consequently, our question shifts from asking what these verses say about me and my life to what this passage says about God and His story, and then how we fit into that overall narrative.

Jesus is the main character in Scripture. He is the center of the story. Everything revolves around Him.

How does understanding that the entire Bible is the story of Jesus change the way you approach reading it?

What are some areas of your life that you need to fight to remember that Jesus holds all things together?

Man Sins

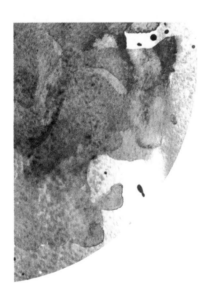

Introducing the Study

In the beginning, there was God and nothing else. He has co-existed in the Persons of the Father, Son, and Holy Spirit from all eternity. Furthermore, it was through the Son and for the Son that all things were created good, and through Him all things hold together even today.

 What happens when we begin to drift from remembering it is through the Son and for the Son that all things were created and hold together?

Unfortunately, what was created good did not stay in its perfect order. While the world around us might look at earthquakes, cancer, tsunamis, poverty, and the like and call them tragedies, disasters, or just cruel twists of fate, Christians look to the storyline of the Bible and see the ultimate source of these calamities—sin.

Do you think it's correct to attribute all that's wrong in the world to sin? Why or why not?

Setting the Context

God's creation was good; very good, in fact. The first man and woman lived together in God's garden where He had placed them, and they did the good work of representing His image in creation and living in harmonious relationship with Him and one another.

 How does the relational nature of the triune God impact your understanding of why He created people?

It's at this point in the story that we are introduced to another character—**the serpent**—who was not content with his place in creation. He did not want to serve God as Creator but instead wanted to be God himself. Not only that, this creature desired that people—God's prized creation—would adopt the same self-determining attitude and throw off the loving rule and reign of God. So **he tempted the first humans** to violate the one prohibition God had lovingly given them—do not eat from the *one* forbidden tree.

Adam and Eve did choose to eat from that tree and set in motion **a downward spiral of sin** we see graphically depicted in Genesis 3–11.

How would you define *sin*?

Ultimately sin became so great on earth that God decided to wipe creation clean with a worldwide flood. But in His grace, God made a way for His judgment of the wicked to lead to the salvation of Noah and his family. **"Salvation Through Judgment"** (p. 23) shows how this event foreshadows the cross of Jesus Christ and God's eternal plan of rescue for His people, for those who believe in His Son.

✚ CHRIST Connection

Our sin reveals the depth of our rebellion against God and our helplessness to do anything to be right with God again. But what we cannot do, God has done through Jesus. Jesus is the Son of Eve whom God graciously provided to crush the head of the serpent Satan and rescue us from sin and death (Gen. 3:15).

Salvation *Through Judgment*

JUDGMENT	THE EVENT	THE MEANS	SALVATION
The Wicked	*The Flood (Gen. 6:9)*	*Floodwater*	Noah and His Family
The Egyptians	*The Exodus (Ex. 1–15)*	*The Plagues and the Red Sea*	The Israelites
Judah and Jerusalem	*The Exile (2 Chron. 36)*	*The Babylonians*	The Remnant
Sinners/ Jesus Christ	*The Cross (Rom. 5)*	*God's Wrath and Our Substitute*	Believers in Christ
God's Enemies	*The Final Judgment (2 Thess. 1)*	*God's Wrath and Hell*	God's People

Continuing the Discussion

▶ Watch this session's video, and then continue the group discussion using the following guide.

What images or phrases about sin were most striking to you in the video? Why?

How does sin keep us from fulfilling our mission as image bearers of our Creator God?

As a group, read Genesis 3:1-7.

Look closely at the serpent's words. What was he implying about the nature and character of God through this temptation?

What are some of the noticeable effects of sin you see in this passage?

✳ What can we learn about our own sin from the serpent's temptation and Adam and Eve's response?

Sin is much more than a choice about a piece of fruit; it is a failure to trust in the good character and rule of God. As a result of sin, our relationship with God and with others is fractured beyond our ability to repair.

As a group, read Genesis 6:5-8.

What do these verses reveal about the gravity and seriousness of sin?

How does this passage show both the reality of judgment and the hope of being saved?

✱ How should the reality of God's judgment motivate us?

The Bible tells us the consequences of sin are death and judgment. Because of this, we should put our full faith in God alone to save, but we must also strive to help others see the consequences of sin and how they might also be saved from God's judgment.

As a group, read Genesis 11:1-9.

Does God's reaction in this story surprise you? Why or why not?

How did the people's work demonstrate a prideful disobedience?

✱ Why is sin, at its core, an exercise in pride?

The people in this account wanted to replace God with themselves, taking the glory that is rightfully due to Him. At its core, sin is always an effort at self-rule and self-determination in which we reject the loving authority of God our Creator.

 # MISSIONAL Application

Record in this space at least one way you will apply the truth of Scripture as a sinner who knows of the grace of God in Jesus Christ.

Personal Study 1

Man's sin ruptured our relationship with God and others.

Read Genesis 3:1-7.

In the garden of Eden, God had provided everything Adam and Eve would ever need. His only prohibition for the first couple was they could not eat from one particular tree. This rule was not arbitrary; He told them not to eat from that one tree because their disobedience would result in death. God wanted Adam and Eve to believe Him, to believe in His goodness, for their well-being. But Satan—a mysterious figure who opposes God—slithered onto the scene through the serpent. And the serpent planted a serious and grave lie into the heart of Eve.

Satan knew that if he wanted Eve to sin, he would need to make her doubt if she could really trust God. So he convinced her that God was holding out on her—He was not giving Eve something that was good. This is the true evil behind the temptation; ultimately, it was a question regarding the character of God and whether He could be trusted, not just about whether a piece of fruit was good to eat.

Satan put the idea in Eve's mind that God wanted her to stay away from the tree not so she wouldn't die but because He didn't want her to truly live. To this point, God had provided for her every need, but for the first time, Eve was confronted with the possibility that there might be more for her outside of God's will than within it.

Adam and Eve chose to rebel against God by eating the fruit. With this choice, our first parents plunged humanity and the rest of creation into darkness. In eating the fruit, they rebelled against God's authority and goodness and chose the road of self-lordship over trusting God.

Before the sin of Adam and Eve, God had determined what was good. But when they took that forbidden bite, the first humans declared they were going to decide what was good for them. They didn't want God to tell them what was best for them; He couldn't be trusted anymore, and it was no longer His place to decide. Instead, Adam and Eve, and all their descendants, would determine their own courses of action. In that moment, we grasped for the authority that belonged to God, our Creator, and tried to take it for ourselves. We decided to be our own gods.

Our disobedience didn't stop with the rejection of God's authority; we also turned our backs on the primary reason for our existence—relationship with God. A loving relationship had existed between God and His image bearers. But after our rejection, humans no longer saw God as the near and intimate Father they had once known so well. Instead of reveling in God's presence, Adam and Eve ran and hid from God, and we continue to do the same. We too live estranged from God, thinking that if we obey Him, we will miss out on something better—something good He wants to withhold from us. We see God as being out to sabotage our happiness and joy.

Furthermore, sin ruptured the relationship between Adam and Eve. From the very moment of their eating, new elements entered into that relationship, elements of distrust, of blame, and of accusation. The first couple went from being naked and unashamed—no barriers between them and complete acceptance and intimacy—to being clothed and ashamed.

Our act of sin in Adam and Eve was not primarily about a piece of fruit. It was about exchanging God for an idol. In eating the forbidden fruit, we were essentially saying to God, "Anyone or anything but You!" trusting in a creature instead of the Creator. As a result, we are broken. This brokenness is most clearly seen in the fracturing of relationships that God had established for His image bearers, and we still feel the effects today.

What are some of the ways sin continues to affect your relationship with God?

How does sin impact your relationships with others?

Personal Study 2

Humanity's sin grieves God and brings judgment.

Read Genesis 6:5-8.

Eating the fruit in the garden and the rejection of God it symbolized threw all of creation into upheaval. As the story continues, we see sin spiraling out of control just a few chapters later. Things weren't getting better but much, much worse. The one act of disobedience was not an anomaly; now "every inclination of the human mind was nothing but evil all the time" (6:5). And this growing sinfulness didn't just impact us. The author of Genesis tells us God was "deeply grieved" by the evil of humanity (6:6).

What we see from the grieving of God's heart is something very unique: The all-powerful Being who created the universe voluntarily (and that is an important distinction) bound His heart with man when He formed him with His hands. We weren't just made in God's image; we received His love and heartfelt affection. So our idolatry and rebelliousness, then, is like a knife in His back, a knife to the heart! Though we are about to see how holy God must respond to sin and punish it severely, we must remember this "grief" along with His righteous anger. God justly judges sin, yet His unfailing love manifests itself through His glorious grace. We see this in the story of Noah.

While he deserved to perish under God's waters of judgment with the rest of humanity, Noah found favor, or grace, in the eyes of the Lord. That is why salvation was extended to him, not because of anything he had done. Noah was not righteous by his own merit but by the grace given to him by God. Notice also that salvation went beyond Noah and extended to the members of his family. The righteousness of Noah was the foundation of the preservation of the rest of his family.

Does that sound like anyone else you know? The story of Noah points ahead to Jesus. In Noah we see a pattern, a shadow, for how God will offer salvation from sin. Jesus is the One in whom God is truly pleased, the One God truly favors. Though all have sinned and fallen short of the glory of God (Rom. 3:23), though none are righteous, not even one (Rom. 3:10), based solely upon the person of Jesus, His work and His righteousness, God offers us salvation.

Noah's family was saved not on the basis of their righteousness but on the basis of Noah's righteousness, and that by God's grace. They were saved because they belonged to Noah. Likewise, we're not saved by our own works but by the work of Jesus alone, and we will be saved from God's coming judgment because we belong to Jesus.

Through the story of the flood, we see the gospel framed as salvation through judgment. What does this mean? While the entire world was turning from God and rejecting Him—telling Him they didn't trust Him, just like their parents before them—Noah was building an ark. He was demonstrating through his obedience that he believed God. He had faith that God was going to do what He had said. And the waters of judgment did come.

The same water that swallowed up everyone who didn't believe in the word of God lifted Noah up. As the waters increased, everyone else was pressed down and crushed. But at the same time, Noah and his family were lifted up and saved. The waters of judgment actually saved him; it was salvation through judgment. And Peter confirmed this for us later in the Bible: "God patiently waited in the days of Noah while the ark was being prepared. In it a few—that is, eight people—were saved *through* water" (1 Pet. 3:20, italics added).

Surprisingly, the waters were actually salvation for some and death for others. In the biblical storyline, the reality of salvation through judgment will be seen most gloriously in the cross of Jesus Christ. As Jesus was judged on the cross for our sin, we were being saved. Salvation came to us through the very instrument by which death came to Jesus. God judges sin and wickedness, but He brings salvation out of this judgment.

What is the significance of "grief" preceding God's judgment of sinful people?

What picture of God do we have when we consider His anger apart from His grief? What about when we think of God as grieving but never angry? Why is it important to hold these two truths together?

Personal Study 3

Humanity's sin reveals our prideful disobedience.

Read Genesis 11:1-9.

We might think that so drastic a judgment and such an amazing salvation in the flood would renew humanity's trust in God and foster deeper reverence and worship. But soon after the flood, we see the evidence of sin resurface and the pattern of sin continue. When we reach chapter 11, we see prideful disobedience on display through the construction of the city and tower of Babylon, also known as Babel.

At the tower of Babylon, humans gathered around a common mission, united as one people. Their focus on a shared mission actually brought them together in such a way that God said nothing was impossible for them. This sounds great, right? A step in the right direction? Wrong. The common mission that united the people at the tower of Babylon was the idea that they could make a great name for themselves, not for God. They were unwilling to resound with the praises of God's great name and were united in their rejection of Him—united in one mind and purpose in prideful disobedience.

So we see God come down and further isolate humankind from one another by confusing their language. Yet even here there is an element of mercy in this act of judgment. By confusing their language, God slowed down the horrible developments that followed in the wake of human sinfulness.

Sin has affected everything. It has broken every relationship we have—with God, human beings, and creation. We need a better solution than Adam, but what hope do we have? The Scripture teaches us that in Adam all sinned (Rom. 5:12). You and I wouldn't have acted any differently if we had been in the garden with the serpent.

Yes, all of our individual acts of sin are very real and very serious. And yes, our individual acts of sin contribute to our guilt before God, but our problem goes even deeper than that. Sin is not just what we do. We *are* sinners, this is who we are, and we cannot save ourselves.

We have a sinful nature because Adam is our head. The only solution is a new head. Our old head brings death; we need a new head that will give us life. The good news of the gospel is that a new head has been offered to us in Christ Jesus (Rom. 5:17-19). God has adopted us through Jesus so that in the place of our prideful disobedience and judgment, He may grant us every spiritual blessing. Through Him we are holy and blameless because that is the inheritance we receive under the headship of Jesus.

God is bringing back the humanity that our sin has broken. He is restoring us to a state even better than our original creation, to a state as authentic and perfected humans who bear His image. Our relationship with God is remedied through Jesus. And our reconciliation with God also affects our relationships with other people.

When we repent and believe in Christ, we are forgiven and accepted by God. This truth must affect the way we treat others. When a brother or sister in Christ wrongs us and we desire to enact our own judgment against them, we are saying that the price Jesus paid for that sin on the cross was not enough. We are asking them to pay a little more because somewhere deep in our hearts, we believe the authority we hold as an offended party is greater than God's. Instead, we must freely offer forgiveness and pardon, just as we have been forgiven and pardoned.

The restoration of our relationship to God and our relationship to others means the church is the inverse of Babylon. We gather not to make a great name for ourselves but to make known the glorious name of Jesus Christ. We go out into the world on mission not to spread the news of our personal kingdoms but to spread the presence of the unfailing, never-ending kingdom of God.

Why is it impossible to seek God's glory and our own glory at the same time?

How can we show the world we desire God's fame rather than the glory of our own names?

God Makes a Covenant with Abraham

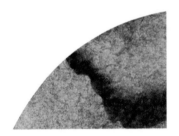

Introducing the Study

Paul lamented in Romans 3:10 that "there is no one righteous, not even one." Since the fall in the garden of Eden, we are all sinners and rebels against our good Creator, both by our inherited nature and by our choices.

> **Where have you observed the effects of sin, both in you and in the world, this week?**

The just punishment for this cosmic rebellion of which we are all a part is death—eternal separation from the God who created us and loves us. And yet through Christ, God Himself has paid the price we owe for our sin. In His glorious plan of redemption, God has done what we could not do. He Himself is both just and the One who justifies sinners (Rom. 3:26), and His desire is that every nation and every people group on earth be blessed through the good news that they can be saved through faith.

 Why is it important that we come to see and fully embrace God's global mission?

Setting the Context

Genesis 3–11 is a downward spiral of humankind's sin where we see the devastating and far-reaching effects of the rebellion that began in Eden. This culminated in the judgment of Babylon and **the shattering and scattering of humanity** throughout the earth.

> ✱ What results would you expect from a people divided based on language and eventually culture and race?

Though humanity was now divided, hope remained for a rescue from sin, and this hope was communicated next through, of all things, a genealogy introducing us to another character in the unfolding drama of Scripture—**Abram**.

Very little is known about Abram's early life. He and his wife, Sarai, were childless (Gen. 11:30). He may have been a shepherd, and he was from the city of Ur (vv. 28,31). But God called this obscure man to be a pivotal piece in His plan of redemption, the first piece in reversing the curse of Babylon, for God planned to bless him and his descendants in a unique way. **"Abram's Journey"** (p. 35) shows the location of Ur and Abram's journey to a new land, which involved passing by and leaving behind Babylon.

Not only would God bless Abram in tangible form but the entire world would also be blessed through him as the father of the Jewish people, through whom would come **his descendant Jesus**.

✝ CHRIST Connection

God promised Abraham that He would bless the world through his descendants. Jesus Christ is the promised descendant of Abraham through whom salvation flows to the world.

Abram's *Journey*

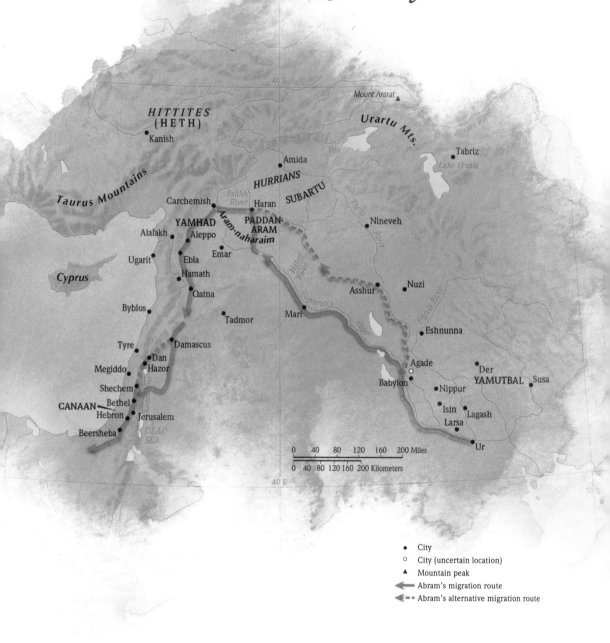

HITTITES
(HETH)
Kanish

Taurus Mountains

Urartu Mts.

Mount Ararat ▲

Araxes River

Tabriz
Lake Urmia

Lake Van

Amida

HURRIANS

Carchemish   Haran   SUBARTU

Balikh River

Tigris River

Nineveh

YAMHAD

Aram-naharaim

PADDAN-ARAM

Alalakh   Aleppo
Ugarit   Ebla   Emar

Cyprus

Hamath

Qatna

Byblos

Tadmor

Mari

Habol River

Euphrates River

Asshur   Nuzi

Eshnunna

Diyala River

Tyre   Damascus

Megiddo   Dan
Hazor

Shechem

CANAAN   Bethel
Hebron   Jerusalem

Beersheba

DEAD SEA

Agade
Babylon   Der   YAMUTBAL   Susa
Nippur
Isin   Lagash
Larsa
Ur

40 E

40 E

50 E

0   40   80   120   160   200 Miles
0   40 80 120 160 200 Kilometers

• City
○ City (uncertain location)
▲ Mountain peak
⬅ Abram's migration route
⬅= = Abram's alternative migration route

Continuing the Discussion

▶ Watch this session's video, and then continue the group discussion using the following guide.

For you, what aspect of Abraham's life and faith stuck out the most from the video? Why?

What does the covenant God made with Abraham reveal about His nature and character?

As a group, read Genesis 12:1-4.

If you were Abram, how do you think you would have responded to such a call from God? What might have been some of your hesitations or objections?

✳ What does Abram's response reveal about his faith and about the nature of faith in general?

What was God's ultimate purpose in initiating this covenant with Abram? Why is this important to recognize in terms of salvation history and our lives as well?

God called Abram to leave all he knew and go to a new place He would eventually reveal to him. Abram demonstrated faith by responding positively, though he didn't know the specifics of God's call. God's plan was to make a covenant with Abram and use him as a vessel through whom He would bless all the nations of the earth.

As a group, read Genesis 15:1-6.

Why was Abram struggling with the promises of God in these verses?

✳ What are some ways that we, like Abram, try to take matters into our own hands?

Look particularly at verse 6. Why is this verse so important?

Many years passed between Genesis 12 and 15, and despite God's promise, Abram was still childless. God reminded Abram that He would keep His promises, and Abram believed God. It was through faith that Abram was counted righteous, just as we are counted righteous today through faith in Christ.

As a group, read Genesis 17:1-10.

> When have you felt like Abraham, needing to be reminded of God's promises?

> How did God set apart Abraham and his offspring in this passage?

✳ In what ways does God call Christians to be set apart today?

God set apart His people through the act of circumcision. The people of faith today are set apart through what the New Testament calls a circumcision "of the heart" (Rom. 2:29), whereby we believe in Christ.

✝ MISSIONAL Application

Record in this space at least one way you will apply the truth of Scripture as one who recognizes that God credits righteousness to those who believe in His Son, Jesus Christ.

Personal Study 1

God initiates a renewed relationship with human beings.

Read Genesis 12:1-4.

As we saw in the previous session, Genesis 11 tells the story of the generations who came out of the flood and settled in a valley in the land of Shinar and began building the tower of Babylon (or Babel), intending for its top to reach into the sky. The Lord came down and judged their self-exaltation and rebellion by scattering them over the earth.

The problem of sin and separation from God that began in the garden in Genesis 3 had not gotten better; it had only gotten worse. Much worse. People were not only separated from God, but they also were separated from one another.

What can be done about these barriers between God and one another? What can we do to fix what is now broken? Well, as we have seen over and over in the story already, we cannot do anything, but God can. He had already promised that an offspring from Eve would crush the serpent's head (Gen. 3:15). The line through which this One would come went through Seth and then Noah. And in Genesis 12, God revealed this rescuer would come through Abram and his family—a new people He would form.

In Genesis 12:1-4, God initiated a renewed relationship with His image bearers. Notice in these verses how many times the pronoun "I" appears in the Lord's declaration to Abram. This shows us that God is the initiator of this covenant. The promise and hope of salvation comes from Him, not from us.

Through Abram's descendants—and more specifically through one descendant, Jesus—God will reverse the misfortunes of Eden (separation from God) and Babylon (separation from each other). The people of Babylon wanted to "make a name" for themselves (Gen. 11:4), but God promised to make Abram's name great (12:2). The rebels at Babylon were scattered over the earth under God's judgment, but God promised through Abram to bless "all the peoples on earth" (12:3).

God will reverse the tragedy of our sin by means of a covenant relationship with Abram, in which He made three promises to him. God promised Abram land, offspring, and blessing.

First, He promised Abram land, and in connection with that, He commanded Abram to leave his own land and travel to another land God would show him. This text ends with Abram obeying God's command and leaving Haran for Canaan—the promised land. Abram's obedience was an expression of his faith in God's promise.

Second, God promised offspring when He said He would make Abram into a great nation. This promise continued the promise of Genesis 3:15. At several key points, God refers to Abram's "offspring," or "seed" (15:5; 17:8), and this promise becomes the primary focus of the stories about Abram in Genesis. At the point when God established this covenant, and for many years after, Abram and his wife, Sarai, remained childless, which greatly stretched their faith in this promise of God.

Finally, God promised to bless all the peoples on earth through Abram and his offspring, a promise that sets the stage for the rest of history. God's plan is to seek and save the lost—all the peoples of the earth, not just a few. He wants to be Lord in covenant relationship with a people comprised of those from all the nations on earth. From Abram would come the Israelites, who were called not to receive God's blessings merely for themselves but to be a light to the nations, drawing them to worship the one true and living God.

From the beginning, God's relationship with Abram required Abram to obey God's calling. Why do you think Abram obeyed God by leaving his land?

What would it take for you to obey God if He called you to do something that made no sense from the world's perspective?

Personal Study 2

God commands His people to trust in His promises.

Read Genesis 15:1-6.

God had made wonderful promises of a family to Abram, but for many years after, he and Sarai remained childless. Both of them were old, with Sarai being well past the years of child-bearing. In the years following God's first promise of a family, Abram had moved to different lands, separated from his family, and fought battles, but still there was no child. Abram didn't just lack the large family God had promised, he didn't even have a single son to carry on his family's name.

Abram looked at God's promise and his situation—namely, his old age—and he figured it was time to press into God. That is why he mentioned his servant Eliezer, the present heir of his household. Did God intend for His promises to flow through Abram's slave? Hardly seems like the start of a great nation in his great name. If we're honest, we'll admit there are times when the promises of God do not look so promising, and we struggle to continue on in belief.

In God's kindness, however, even in the midst of Abram's doubt, He came to him and restated the promises, even adding to them. And Abram believed!

God reassured Abram that Eliezer would not be his heir; he would have a son of his own. God would give Abram more than that, though. He would give offspring as numerous as the stars in the sky. Not only did God restate this promise to Abram and his children repeatedly (see Gen. 22:17; 26:4; also 28:14), but He also brought it to fruition, beginning with the birth of Isaac (see Deut. 1:10; 10:22).

So again Abram believed the promise of God, and God counted it to him as righteousness. In Galatians 3, the apostle Paul pointed to Abram's faith as a model of saving faith. Paul argued that we are not justified (i.e., declared righteous before God) by trying to keep the rules (Gal. 3:11). Those who break God's law are cursed, and we're all law-breakers. But the good news is that Christ became that curse for us on the cross (v. 13). Justification only comes through faith in Jesus, and as with Abram, God credits His righteousness to our account (vv. 6-7). Today, we too are called to trust the promises of God.

Those who share Abram's faith are the true sons of Abraham (Rom. 4:11-12; Gal. 3:7). And they will be an innumerable multitude in heaven from every people group on the planet (i.e., as numerous as the stars of the sky; cf. Rev. 7).

The Lord made this promise to Abram and then showed Abram He was bound to keep it by means of a covenant ceremony with Abram (like a marriage ceremony). Genesis 15:7-21 gives this account. God commanded Abram to bring Him animals and to cut them in half (except for the birds, 15:10). Abram fell into a deep sleep, and the Lord told him about the future exodus from Egypt as well as the conquest of all the peoples in the promised land. Then the presence of the Lord, represented in a smoking fire pot and a flaming torch, passed between the animal corpses. This act was, in effect, God saying to Abram, "Let this happen to Me if these things do not come true. Let Me be cut in pieces if I don't uphold My end of the covenant." The Lord was willing to take the covenant curses upon Himself if the covenant were broken. And because humanity as a whole failed to obey, that is exactly what He ended up doing at the cross, when Jesus took our curse of sin upon Himself.

In what areas of life are you prone to struggle with trusting the promises of God (financial, marital, parental, relational, etc.)? In what ways have you taken matters into your own hands in an attempt to ensure the outcome you want?

How can we resist this tendency to distrust God and try to manufacture our desired results in life?

Personal Study 3

God desires for His people to be set apart for His glory.

Read Genesis 17:1-10.

Abram's faith faltered again as he and Sarai grew older and they still did not have a child. And again God came to him to reiterate the promises and His covenant commitment to Abram. This time, however, He gave Abram a new name, and He gave him a sign of their covenant relationship, a sign that would set His people apart from the rest of the world.

The Lord called Abram to walk blamelessly before Him, and then He restated the promise that He would multiply Abram's offspring and that he would be the father of many nations. So the Lord changed Abram's name to "Abraham," which means "father of a multitude" (v. 5). Not only that, but kings would come from Abraham's family (v. 6). He would produce a royal line leading, of course, to the King of kings—Jesus of Nazareth.

Thus, God will keep His promises, but Abraham had a responsibility to be blameless before God. The covenant was conditionally unconditional! It will come about, but one of Abraham's offspring will have to be blameless. All of them fall short, all of them except for Jesus Christ.

You might remember, if you grew up in church, singing a song called "Father Abraham." That song was sort of the Christian version of "The Hokey Pokey." Aside from the goofy "right arm, left arm, right foot, left foot," it had some great theology because the song taught "Gentile" children that being a child of Abraham has nothing to do with your race and everything to do with faith in Jesus.

Through faith in Christ, the nations are becoming the children of Abraham.

The Lord's covenant relationship with Abraham gives rise to one of the key phrases in the entire Bible when God promised to be the God of Abraham's offspring. As the saying goes, "I will be their God, and they will be My people" (cf. Jer. 24:7; 31:33; 32:38; Ezek. 11:20; 14:11; 37:23,27; Zech. 8:8; 2 Cor. 6:16; Heb. 8:10). This is a committed relationship. God promised unconditionally to make these things a reality through Abraham and his offspring. He would not forsake them. They will always be His people (like a husband who commits to be faithful to his bride always).

In Genesis 17, God gave the sign of the covenant between Himself and Abraham, one that Abraham and his offspring were to keep as an everlasting covenant—male circumcision. Every male would be circumcised as a sign of participation in the covenant. This outward symbol marked out in the flesh those who belonged to the people of God, setting them apart from all the other peoples of the world. And there is a reason circumcision was given—it marked out the place from which the seed comes. Keeping this covenant was a serious matter because anyone who was not circumcised would be cut off from the people (i.e., not part of God's people).

In order to be a true blessing to the nations, the children of God would need to maintain their distinction from the world. The same is true for us today. We are to be set apart from the rest of the world, not by physical circumcision but by the circumcision of the heart (Rom. 2:29). Our lives should bear the marks of God's redeeming grace.

What does being part of God's chosen people by faith teach us about the nature of God's love for us?

Can we be on mission with God and yet fail to pursue holiness? Why or why not?

God Tests Abraham

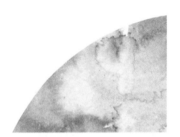

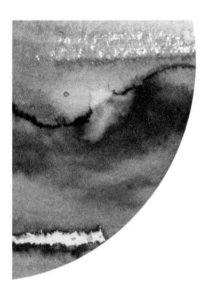

Introducing the Study

Beginning with Abraham, God set apart a people on the earth whom He would uniquely bless. From this line would come Jesus, and ultimately through Him, God would bless all the peoples of the world with salvation from sin—bringing back together through faith in the gospel what had been separated through sin.

 How should remembering God's plan to bless the whole world through Abraham's descendants frame the way we live each day?

Although God's promises seemed so distant and unbelievable at times, Abraham believed God. This is the single most important statement that marked his life, and yet, his biggest test of faith was yet to come. God would indeed make good on His promise to give Abraham a son, and that son, Isaac, would be at the center of that test—the defining moment of his faith. Through this test we see not only a great demonstration of faith but also a shadow of God's own sacrifice as a Father.

 Why do you think God tested Abraham's faith even though he had already shown he believed in God?

Setting the Context

After long years of waiting, struggles, and doubts, Genesis 17 leaves Abraham with **renewed confidence** in God's promise of an heir and also **a physical sign of the covenant**, a reminder of God's faithfulness—circumcision. And yet, the waiting still was not over. One more year would pass between Genesis 17 and 21, where the birth of Isaac is recorded.

Abraham had another son, Ishmael through Hagar, Sarah's maidservant (Gen. 16), but God's promise of offspring would come specifically through Sarah (17:19-22). And the Lord miraculously provided this "only son" of promise. **"The LORD Will Provide"** (p. 47) shows just a glimpse of the Lord's desire to provide for His people.

> How has the Lord provided for you?

When Abraham was one hundred years old, his son through Sarah was finally born. God's long-promised blessing of descendants to Abraham was at last visibly being fulfilled in Isaac, and Abraham was faithful to mark this **son of the covenant** in the way God had commanded him with circumcision, the sign of the covenant.

We don't know how old Isaac was when Genesis 22 opens, but it's clear from his interactions with his father that a number of years had gone by. The treasured little boy, Abraham's "only son," had grown, and God was about to use him in **the greatest test of Abraham's faith**.

> How has the Lord tested you?

✚ CHRIST Connection

Isaac's question "Where is the lamb for the sacrifice?" echoes through the pages of the Old Testament and is ultimately answered at the beginning of the New Testament when John the Baptist sees Jesus of Nazareth and declares, "Behold the Lamb!"

The LORD *Will Provide*

	SUBJECT TO DEATH	THE SUBSTITUTE	THE REASON
Genesis 22	Isaac, Abraham's "only son" (Gen. 22:2)	A Ram	"And Abraham named that place The LORD Will Provide, so today it is said: 'It will be provided on the LORD's mountain.'" (Gen. 22:14)
Exodus 12–13 (The Passover)	The Firstborn Sons of Israel	An Unblemished Lamb or Goat	"The blood on the houses where you are staying will be a distinguishing mark for you; when I see the blood, I will pass over you." (Ex. 12:13)
Leviticus 16 (The Day of Atonement)	Israel	Animals, Including a Ram	"Atonement will be made for you on this day to cleanse you, and you will be clean from all your sins before the LORD." (Lev. 16:30)
Revelation 5	Sinners	Jesus, "the Lamb of God" (John 1:29)	"You [the Lamb] were slaughtered, and you purchased people for God by your blood from every tribe and language and people and nation." (Rev. 5:9)

Continuing the Discussion

▶ Watch this session's video, and then continue the group discussion using the following guide.

How do tests reveal the nature and substance of our faith?

How is the gospel foreshadowed in this story?

As a group, read Genesis 22:1-6.

How do you think you would have responded to this call from God if you were Abraham?

✳ How would you define *faith* based on this test from the Lord?

Where do you see Abraham demonstrating faith in God in these verses?

God knew very well what He was asking Abraham to do—to sacrifice the son of promise. In His call, God noted that this was Abraham's "only son Isaac, whom you love." Once again, Abraham proved faithful not only in His obedience to God's command but in telling the servants, "We'll come back to you."

As a group, read Genesis 22:7-14.

What stands out most to you about Abraham's actions in these verses?

✳ Why was this such an important demonstration of Abraham's faith?

In what ways do you see a foreshadowing of the death of Jesus in these verses?

Based on what we see here, Abraham had every intention of sacrificing his son. The knife was raised, but then God intervened and prevented Abraham from following through. While Abraham was spared from sacrificing his son, it's important to notice that the sacrifice was still made—God provided a substitute. Centuries later, God Himself would lead His own Son up the hill at Calvary, but this time, no substitute for a beloved Son would be provided. This time, that Son, Jesus, would be sacrificed as *the substitute* for the sins of the world.

As a group, read Hebrews 11:17-19.

> According to these verses, what did Abraham believe about God?

 As Christians, why must we believe in God in the same way as Abraham?

These verses help us see the depth of Abraham's faith. Abraham believed that even if he sacrificed Isaac, God would raise him from the dead. He believed God was powerful enough to do this and also that God would keep His promise to raise up generations of descendants through Isaac. For Abraham, the only reasonable outcome of this puzzling test was resurrection. As Christians, the core of our faith rests on the same thing—that God raises the dead, most specifically, that He raised up Jesus and that one day we will be raised as well.

MISSIONAL Application

Record in this space at least one way you will apply the truth of Scripture as one who believes in the resurrection power of the Lord, both physically and spiritually.

Personal Study 1

God calls for a special sacrifice.

Read Genesis 22:1-6.

In the chapters between the previous session and this one, several situations arose in Abraham's life, including a threat to the fulfillment of God's promise when a king named Abimelech attempted to take Sarah as his wife. But God remained faithful, protected Abraham and Sarah, and miraculously provided a son named Isaac (Gen. 21). Isaac was the child of promise; he was the heir through whom the promises would be carried forward.

Some years later, however, Abraham's faith was put to the test. God told Abraham to do something that would horrify any father, but especially the father of the promised son, the first descendant of a family through whom the salvation of the world was to come. This was where the rubber would meet the road for Abraham.

It's easy to say we trust someone, but the proof of that trust is demonstrated through our acts of obedience. Deep trust revealed in obedience is what we see in this story with Abraham. Here the covenant-making God tested Abraham's faith by telling him to sacrifice his "only son Isaac" on one of the mountains in the land of Moriah. The promise of offspring as plentiful as the stars was again in jeopardy as God instructed Abraham to sacrifice his lone descendant.

How would you feel if God were to ask you to sacrifice one of your children? It is beyond imagination. We can't process loving and caring for a child—a gift from God—and then hearing God say, "Go sacrifice your little girl you love on a mountain."

For Abraham, though, this command from God affected much more than his family; it presented a cosmic problem. It was not merely a matter of Abraham waiting decades to have a son through Sarah and then being forced to part with the young man. It was even bigger. God's promise to Abraham did not end with that one son; He had promised Abraham offspring as numerous as the stars and that this offspring would restore the world. The death of Isaac meant the death of this promise of rescuing the world. God's testing us in this way would challenge our faith in Him to provide for us; God's testing of Abraham challenged his faith in God to provide salvation for the world.

When the time came, in obedient faith, Abraham rose early in the morning, gathered the materials for a sacrifice, and set out for the place where God told him to go. After a three-day journey, Abraham saw the place and told his servants to remain with the donkey. He said that he and the boy would go over to the mountain to worship and then return. So Abraham took the wood and laid it on Isaac, he himself carried the fire and the knife, and they set off for the mountain.

Abraham demonstrated strong faith in the promises of God. Not only did he intend to sacrifice Isaac, but he also believed that somehow the boy would come away alive on the other side. After all, he told his servants that after the sacrifice was done, "We'll come back to you" (22:5). He believed that God would keep His promise of offspring even if it required resurrection from the dead (cf. Heb. 11:17-19).

Abraham and Isaac headed up the mountain for the sacrifice. Abraham did not know exactly what would happen, but he still trusted in the promises of God.

Like Abraham, we may not know when we are being tested. In what ways does Abraham's story impact our obedience?

When was the last time God tested you?

Personal Study 2

God provides a substitute sacrifice.

Read Genesis 22:7-14.

We are familiar with the concept of a substitute because we are surrounded by them every day: from substitute teachers to substitute players, substitute menu items and substitute sweeteners. These substitutes are important to us because they enable us to do what we could not do without them.

The theme of substitution is at the heart of Christianity, only in a much more powerful way. Our faith hinges on our belief that Jesus died in our place for our sins as our substitute. Because of our sin, we deserved to die, and because God is just, that death was owed. But Jesus stepped into our place and paid the death we could not pay. This beauty of Christ's atoning work is foreshadowed in a startling way in the story of Abraham and Isaac.

Notice what Isaac asked his father: "Where is the lamb for the burnt offering?" Isaac knew he and his father were going to perform a sacrifice, and he knew what was involved. He saw that his father had the knife and fire, and Isaac himself was carrying the wood, but there was something important missing. Where was the animal? Isaac's question echoes through the pages of the Old Testament: *Where is the lamb? How will the sacrifice take place?* Generation after generation asked the same question as they too looked around to see how God would provide the deliverance through Eve's offspring as He had promised.

Abraham answered, "God himself will provide the lamb for the burnt offering." This is the heart of the Christian faith. We believe God provides salvation because He is the One who provides the substitute.

The theme of the substitute lamb runs throughout the pages of Scripture, as we will see in future sessions. At the Passover in Egypt, a lamb's blood was shed as a substitute for the life of the firstborn sons of Israel. That sacrifice caused the destroyer to pass over the homes covered by the substitute lamb's blood and death was withheld. The sacrificial system was established requiring God's people to slaughter animals when they sinned against God and one another. And on the Day of Atonement, animals were put to death and their blood covered the mercy seat in the most holy place to cover the sins of the people for the past year.

All of these stories point forward to the moment when the Lord Jesus Himself, the Lamb who takes away the sins of the world, would die as the ultimate and final sacrifice (cf. 1 Cor. 5:7). God provided His one and only Son as the substitute for the world.

Here in Genesis 22, there is a substitute for Isaac, and it's a ram. Just as Isaac, the willing son to be sacrificed, hints at Jesus—God's Son went up the mountain carrying the wooden cross—so also the ram hints at Jesus as our substitute. The ram caught in the thorns points forward to the coming descendant from Abraham—Jesus the King, who would be crowned with thorns and pierced for our transgressions.

Abraham was right. The Lord would provide a substitute sacrifice. He did so on that fateful day on Mount Moriah. And many years later, the Lord provided a substitute sacrifice for sin on Mount Calvary—Jesus Christ, God's Son.

Why does faith require obedience?

Why is it vital that God provide a substitute for us?

Why is Jesus as our substitute good news, even when we sin?

Personal Study 3

God commands His people to trust in His provision.

Read Hebrews 11:17-19.

The New Testament writer of Hebrews gives us inspired and valuable insight into this event in Abraham's life. He tells us what Abraham was thinking and what motivated his obedience to the Lord.

Hebrews 11 is considered the "Faith Hall of Fame," and in this passage the author praises Abraham's faith. Faith was the means by which Abraham offered up Isaac when the Lord tested him. Abraham had received a promise that his offspring—his heir—would be the one to bring restoration to the world, and even though God's command to sacrifice Isaac looked contrary to that promise, he began to carry it out.

Why did he offer Isaac? He offered Isaac not just because he had faith in God in general but because he had faith specifically in the resurrection from the dead. He believed God was able to raise Isaac from the grave, just as God had been able to bring life out of Sarah's "dead" womb (Gen. 17:15-19; 21:1-5). For this reason, Abraham was able to obey God, even if that obedience was difficult and painful. The patriarch knew that resurrection would ultimately undo all the sorrow and heartache.

The parallels between Abraham's story and the gospel of Jesus are remarkable:

Isaac	Jesus
Abraham's "only" son (of promise)	God's "one and only" Son (John 3:16)
Subject to be sacrificed, and willing	Subject to be sacrificed, and willing
Carried wood for the sacrifice	Carried cross for His sacrifice
"The Lord Will Provide" (Gen. 22:14) God provided a substitute	"The Lamb of God" (John 1:29) God provided the Substitute
Figuratively raised from the dead	Physically raised from the dead

Sacrifice was necessary for sinful humanity to be made right with a holy God. This place where Abraham bound Isaac, Mount Moriah, has traditionally been understood as the site where the temple later would be built, the place where sacrifices were made so that Almighty God could live in the midst of sinful humanity (cf. 2 Chron. 3:1). The ultimate sacrifice that all of these temple sacrifices pointed to was the cross of Jesus Christ. And it was on that cross where the world gazed upon the true answer to Isaac's question—God Himself indeed provided the Lamb.

How does your faith in the resurrection impact the way you obey God?

What are some ways we might try to provide atonement for ourselves when we sin?

Where in your life do you need to trust God more?

God Works Through a Dysfunctional Family

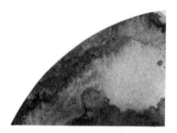

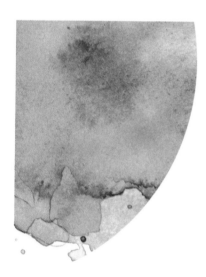

Introducing the Study

"Where is the lamb for the sacrifice?" That question from young Isaac echoes through the entire Old Testament, a question which is ultimately answered with Jesus. In Jesus we find the substitute sacrifice for our sin.

God's plan to provide the substitute for our sin was in motion. But as God formed a people through Abraham's descendants, it quickly became apparent that their disobedience was an issue. Turmoil, favoritism, deception, anger, and sin plagued the family. But through the story of Jacob, Isaac's son and Abraham's grandson, we see that the success of God's plan is not based on the merit of His people but on His power, mercy, and grace.

 Why does God choose unlikely people to advance His plan of redemption?

How is it encouraging to read stories of unlikely recipients of God's mercy and grace?

Setting the Context

As Abraham had predicted, both he and Isaac came down from the mountain. God had provided a substitute sacrifice and spared the life of **the promised son**. God's promise to bless every nation on the earth through Abraham's offspring was intact.

 How did Abraham's knowledge of God's promises and character fuel his faith? What can we learn from that?

Abraham died at the age of 175, but not before he saw his son, Isaac, married to Rebekah, the wife the Lord provided for him. And as God had said, His promises passed on to Isaac. **"The Patriarchs"** (p. 59) traces the promises and their implications through the Book of Genesis.

Just like Sarah, Rebekah was barren until the Lord provided yet again, and Rebekah conceived twins. Surprisingly, before the twins were even born, the Lord had told Rebekah that **the older would serve the younger**, turning the customary privilege of the firstborn on its head.

Not surprisingly, **the two sons clashed** with each other. Esau, the older brother, was a hunter and the favorite of his father, while Jacob stayed closer to home and was the favorite of his mother. Esau was impetuous, and Jacob, a schemer. On one occasion, Jacob tempted his hungry older brother into giving him the birthright—a larger portion of the family inheritance—in exchange for a bowl of stew. But later Jacob and his mother would conspire to take something even more important away from Esau, and the family of promise would be torn apart.

CHRIST Connection

Jacob's story is a good example of why humanity needs a Savior. Like Jacob, we seek a blessing that is not ours, but we cannot lie, deceive, or trick to receive it. Instead, Jesus shared His blessing with us when He took the judgment we deserve so that we might receive the blessing He deserves.

The **Patriarchs**

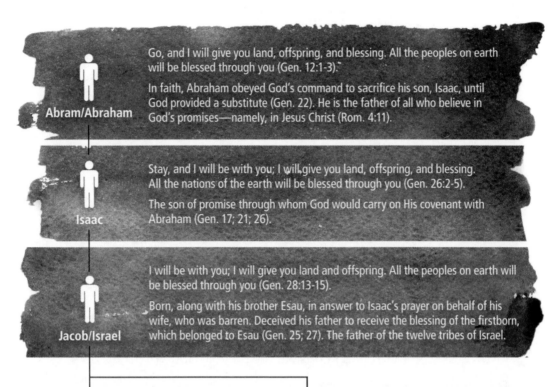

Abram/Abraham

Go, and I will give you land, offspring, and blessing. All the peoples on earth will be blessed through you (Gen. 12:1-3).

In faith, Abraham obeyed God's command to sacrifice his son, Isaac, until God provided a substitute (Gen. 22). He is the father of all who believe in God's promises—namely, in Jesus Christ (Rom. 4:11).

Isaac

Stay, and I will be with you; I will give you land, offspring, and blessing. All the nations of the earth will be blessed through you (Gen. 26:2-5).

The son of promise through whom God would carry on His covenant with Abraham (Gen. 17; 21; 26).

Jacob/Israel

I will be with you; I will give you land and offspring. All the peoples on earth will be blessed through you (Gen. 28:13-15).

Born, along with his brother Esau, in answer to Isaac's prayer on behalf of his wife, who was barren. Deceived his father to receive the blessing of the firstborn, which belonged to Esau (Gen. 25; 27). The father of the twelve tribes of Israel.

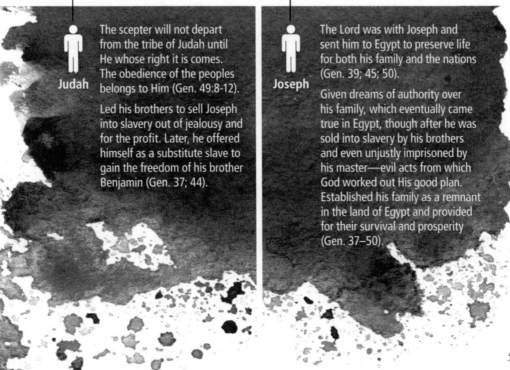

Judah

The scepter will not depart from the tribe of Judah until He whose right it is comes. The obedience of the peoples belongs to Him (Gen. 49:8-12).

Led his brothers to sell Joseph into slavery out of jealousy and for the profit. Later, he offered himself as a substitute slave to gain the freedom of his brother Benjamin (Gen. 37; 44).

Joseph

The Lord was with Joseph and sent him to Egypt to preserve life for both his family and the nations (Gen. 39; 45; 50).

Given dreams of authority over his family, which eventually came true in Egypt, though after he was sold into slavery by his brothers and even unjustly imprisoned by his master—evil acts from which God worked out His good plan. Established his family as a remnant in the land of Egypt and provided for their survival and prosperity (Gen. 37–50).

Continuing the Discussion

 Watch this session's video, and then continue the group discussion using the following guide.

What stuck out to you the most from this video about the dysfunctional family of Isaac? Why?

What can we learn about the plan and purposes of God through His work in this family?

As a group, read Genesis 27:1-10.

Based on these verses, how would you describe the family dynamics at play here?

Are these verses encouraging or discouraging to you? Why?

✳ How should human beings consider their part in God's plan?

These few verses paint a picture of a family in discord. Distrust, deception, greed, and self-promotion plagued the brothers *and* their parents. It's amazing to think that this is the family God chose to be the conduit of His blessing to the earth, and yet, it is encouraging to remember that human sin is no match for the plans and purposes of God. Just as God used this sinful family, He can use us as well.

As a group, read Genesis 27:18-20,25-29.

What can you discern about Jacob's character from these verses?

✳ What do Jacob's actions reveal about the human condition?

How do you see yourself in Jacob?

It might not have been his idea, but Jacob was more than willing to go along with his mother's deceptive plan as long as it benefited him. This is a picture of the human heart, for in our sin we are always prone to choose self-advancement and self-promotion.

As a group, read Genesis 28:10-15.

> Why do you think God gave this particular dream to Jacob? What did He want Jacob to know?

✳ Did Jacob deserve this blessing? Why is that important to know?

Despite all of Jacob's failings, God affirmed His covenant with him. Like Jacob, we are completely dependent upon the mercy and grace of God, especially when it comes to our salvation through the gospel.

✟ MISSIONAL Application

Record in this space at least one way you will apply the truth of Scripture as an unworthy sinner who has received the grace and mercy of God through faith in Jesus Christ.

Personal Study 1

God's plan continues through a dysfunctional family.

Read Genesis 27:1-10.

Some Christians long for "the good old days" when family values were celebrated in our culture. But the truth is what we long for is an illusion, a mirage. There hasn't been an era of "the good old days" since the garden of Eden. Families have always been sinful and dysfunctional. Because of our innate sinfulness, families have always shifted blame, reversed roles, rebelled against God, and much more. This is true today. It was true after the fall. And it was true in "the good old days." Television just didn't show it then.

No family is perfect. Every family has its struggles and challenges. But the good news is that God does not reserve His love, mercy, and grace only for perfect families. He pours it out in abundance on the broken—on all of us. We will see a beautiful picture of this in Isaac's family: God can and does use dysfunctional families to carry out His plans.

When Isaac and Rebekah's children—Esau and Jacob—were in their mother's womb, the Lord told Rebekah that the older would serve the younger. In ancient cultures, the younger son's role was to serve the older son, and the older son would receive the family inheritance. But as this story unfolds, we see the older son, Esau, selling this honor—his birthright—to Jacob for a bowl of stew. Like Adam and Eve in the garden, Esau was defined by food, by his appetite.

Not only did Esau sell his birthright, but he also took Hittite wives. He intermarried with a pagan people who didn't follow the one true God, and his actions made life miserable for his parents (Gen. 26:34-35). But God had declared that His promises to Eve—that her offspring would crush the serpent's head (Gen. 3)—and to Abraham—that his offspring would bring blessing to all the peoples of the earth (Gen. 12)—would be carried forward through Jacob, not Esau.

We see in Genesis 27 a major showdown between these brothers. And even though Isaac and his family were sinful, dysfunctional, and manipulative, God graciously keeps His promises.

Rebekah's plot was to deceive Isaac into thinking that Jacob was Esau. Jacob was to grab goats from their flock so that Rebekah could make a meal that Isaac loved. Jacob protested that even though his father could not see well, if Isaac touched him, then Isaac would realize that he was not Esau. Jacob was concerned that he would be cursed by his father rather than blessed. But Rebekah had everything figured out. She clothed Jacob in Esau's clothes, she put the goats' skin on Jacob to make him hairy like his older brother, and she prepared a meal her husband would like.

Genesis paints an unflattering picture of Abraham and his offspring. We see them lie, cheat, and manipulate. Abraham and Isaac both passed their wives off as their sisters in order to get the heat off themselves (Gen. 12:11-13; 26:7). Isaac and Rebekah both played favorites with their children, as would Jacob. Rebekah and Jacob both were willing to deceive in order to get what they wanted.

But despite all this scheming, God continued to be gracious and kept His promises. His plan to redeem the world would not, and will not, be thwarted by human cunning and sin.

What are some common dysfunctions in families? How can God's grace in the gospel overcome these?

How does the story of God's continual grace through messed-up people free you to be part of His plan?

Personal Study 2

God's plan continues through a deceitful son.

Read Genesis 27:18-29.

Why do we lie and cheat? Usually to get something we want. Because of our sin, we fail to trust God to provide what we need, or we refuse to accept the specific provision He has given to us—just like Adam and Eve way back in Eden. Our discontentment and our self-advancement are just two evidences of the rebellion common to all people. This unending craving for more is in all of us, and it was this craving that drove Jacob to lie to his father, not just once but several times.

Jacob schemed and lied to get what he wanted. He had numerous opportunities to come clean with his father and tell the truth. But he was so blinded by greed for the blessing that he continued to deceive.

We are often no different than Jacob. We too lie, usually because we want something. We want others to have a certain opinion of us, so we "bend" the truth. We want more money for ourselves, so we "massage" the numbers on our tax returns. A craving for a desired outcome fuels lying.

Notice that the words of blessing Isaac uttered over Jacob were basically a restatement of God's promises to his father, Abraham (27:27-29). God had promised Abraham land, offspring, and blessing. Isaac spoke here of land and blessing. He asked that God would cause Jacob's relatives and the nations to serve him. God's blessing would be given to those nations that blessed Jacob, the deceitful younger son.

Of course, this account is not meant to teach us that our conduct doesn't matter. God calls us, as His people, to live with honesty and integrity. But this story does reveal that God works in surprising ways and in surprising people. And every time He does, we are forced to consider two things.

First, we are reminded that God's plan is not thwarted by the evil intentions of the human heart. God has been and is still committed to His plan of redemption through Jesus Christ. No government, no law, no movement, no culture, and no person can stop God from carrying out His plan.

Second, this passage also reminds us that we cannot place limits on the grace and mercy of God. Sometimes we fail to share the good news of Jesus with others because we feel unqualified to do so. We, like Jacob, are full of envy, greed, lies, and sin. Sometimes we fail to share the gospel with others because they, like Jacob, seem out of the reach of God's mercy, hopeless and beyond salvation.

In either case, we are placing limitations on God's power, and as we see in the account of Jacob, those limitations do not exist. Because of God's willingness to work through Jacob, even in his deceit, we should be zealous all the more to speak of His mercy and grace to others, knowing He can use anyone to reach anyone with the gospel.

In what kinds of situations do you find it easiest to lie? What does this teach you about what your heart craves?

How can the desires of the heart be changed? Have you experienced this?

What hope does it give you to know God works even through our deceit and sinfulness to accomplish His plan?

Personal Study 3

God's plan continues through His mercy and grace.

Read Genesis 28:10-15.

Why did God choose to bless Jacob? Certainly not because of Jacob's goodness, righteousness, or merit. Instead, God chose to bless Jacob because of His own mercy and grace. Like Jacob, none of us deserve God's blessing of salvation in Christ. We are all trophies of God's mercy and grace. Our salvation glorifies God because it is dependent exclusively upon Him and His grace.

Because of God's mercy and grace, and for His own glory, God gives us the greatest blessing of all—His presence. Our salvation provides us with many benefits, the foremost of which is being spared from eternal death. But we shouldn't make the mistake of focusing on these benefits and forgetting the greatest blessing of all—God Himself! He will be our God, we will be His people, and we will be together enjoying Him forever. *That* is what is at the center of our salvation.

This promise of God's gracious presence, given to us through His grace and mercy, runs throughout the Bible. We see it here in Genesis 28.

As was foretold at his birth, Jacob received the blessing, even though he stole it from Esau. Afterward, Jacob was forced to flee from his brother's fury. After a day of traveling, Jacob found a place to stay the night and chose a stone as his pillow. As he slept, Jacob dreamed about a stairway on the ground with its top in the heavens. Angels were going up and down on it. It is here that God restated the promises of Abraham and Isaac to Jacob. God reminded Jacob that He is the God of Abraham and Isaac, and He would be Jacob's God too.

The stairway Jacob saw reminds us of the tower of Babylon; its top reached into the sky (see Gen. 11:4). The people of Babylon had attempted to come before God on their own terms. But this story shows us that if human beings are to reconnect with God, we have to first realize we cannot. We don't connect with Him, He connects with us. Our salvation requires God coming down to us. Christianity is different from other religions because we believe God's presence is secured in our lives not through our climbing up toward Him but through His gracious descent toward us.

Genesis 28 shows that God will indeed come to be with His people through Jacob and his offspring. Jacob's stairway gives us a glimpse into the reversal of Babylon. The people of Babylon were trying to get back to God by lifting up a tower, yet it caused them to be separated and scattered all over the planet.

But when *the* offspring of Jacob, God incarnate—Jesus of Nazareth—came down from heaven, He was lifted up to draw all people to Himself. He will bless all the peoples of the earth and reunite them in Himself. John 1:51 tells us that Jesus is the true stairway to heaven. He is the One who reconnects earth and heaven.

Is it possible to experience God's presence and not be changed? Why or why not?

In what ways does sin prohibit us from experiencing the presence of God?

How does God overcome our sin to give us a glimpse of His glory and grace?

God Gives Jacob a New Name

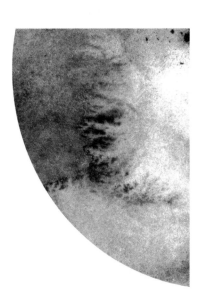
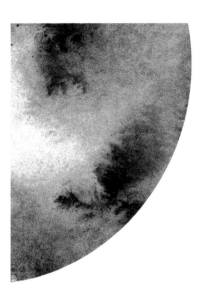

Introducing the Study

Jacob tried to manipulate his way into God's blessing, but the success of God's plan is not based on a person's merit but on God's power, mercy, and grace. Just as Jacob and his dysfunctional family were blessed despite themselves, the gospel reminds us that not one of us is worthy of God's salvation, and yet, not one of us is beyond His grace.

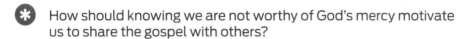 How should knowing we are not worthy of God's mercy motivate us to share the gospel with others?

Jacob's name meant "deceiver," and he lived up to it. But God is not content for His people to remain in their sin. Instead, God works by His grace and mercy not only to save us but to change us for our good and for His glory.

* Why is it important to remember the gospel does not just begin our life with Christ but sustains it as well?

Setting the Context

Jacob had maneuvered his way into receiving the family birthright and the blessing of his father. Making good on His promise from before Jacob and Esau were born, God confirmed **His covenant blessings would indeed pass through Jacob**, even though he was the younger son. But Jacob's choices had left consequences in their wake. His brother, Esau, planned to kill Jacob for his deception.

Knowing the danger, Jacob's mother, Rebekah, sent him away to her brother, Laban, in Haran, where he met **Rachel**, one of his uncle's daughters. Jacob offered to work seven years for Laban for the right to marry Rachel. But Laban was also deceitful, and at the end of seven years, he gave his other daughter, **Leah**, to Jacob as his wife. When Jacob confronted Laban about the deception, Laban offered to give him Rachel as his wife as well, but only if Jacob would work for another seven years. Jacob agreed.

Though Jacob loved Rachel more than Leah, the Lord was kind to Leah and gave her children. This caused much jealousy and bitterness between the sisters, leading to their servants becoming wives as part of a competition, and numerous children were born to Jacob—the next big step in God's plan of a nation coming from Abraham. See **"Jacob's Family"** (p. 71).

Throughout his time working for Laban, God multiplied Jacob's material blessings and he became very rich. The Lord then commanded Jacob to return to the land of his fathers—the land where Esau still lived. With much apprehension, Jacob began the trip home, which led to one night that would define his future.

How do you deal with worry over situations in your life?

✝ CHRIST Connection

God's renaming of individuals in the Old Testament reflects both privilege and responsibility. As Christians, we bear the name of Christ. We receive both the privilege of salvation and the responsibility of mission.

Jacob's *Family*

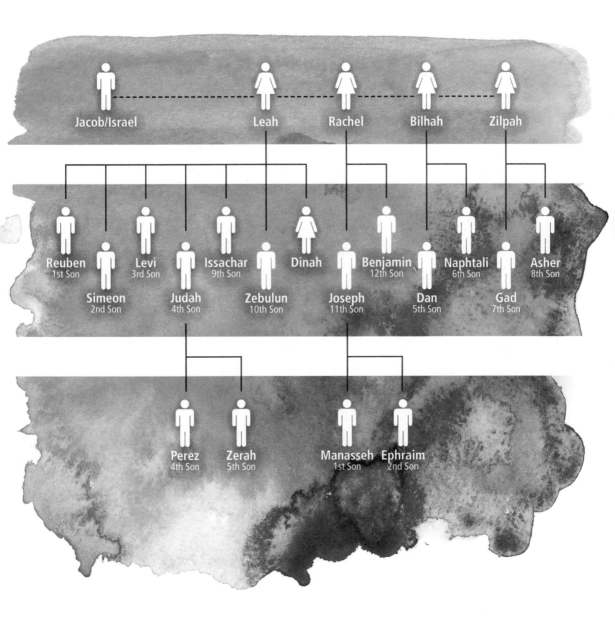

Continuing the Discussion

▶ Watch this session's video, and then continue the group discussion using the following guide.

What are some of the ways we might struggle with God?

How does the renaming of Jacob remind us of what God has done for us in Christ?

As a group, read Genesis 32:24-27.

Have you ever felt as though you were wrestling with God? When and why? What happened as a result?

Was God really not able to win this wrestling match? What was His purpose in wrestling with Jacob?

✳ What does this encounter reveal about God?

Jacob was still trying to use his own abilities to manufacture blessings. In this case, he tried with all his might to hang on to receive something from God. But God was interested in doing something deeper in Jacob's life than Jacob realized. He was interested in forming him into a new person.

As a group, read Genesis 32:28-32.

✳ Why is it significant that God gave Jacob a new name?

What are some ways you have been changed by God through difficult circumstances?

God forced Jacob to own up to his old name and nature. He was a deceiver, but no more. Jacob would have the new name of Israel. This new name was symbolic of both the privilege and responsibility of walking with God. Like Jacob, we have been given new names in Christ—we are no longer strangers, enemies, or rebels; we are now God's children.

As a group, read Genesis 35:9-15.

Why do you think God reminded Jacob of his new name?

✱ What are some times we as Christians also need to be reminded of our new names in Christ?

With the new name of Israel, God was calling Jacob to embrace his identity and purpose as a part of God's plan. When we sin as Christians, it is as if we are forgetting we have been made new in Christ. Fortunately, the Holy Spirit reminds us over and over again that we are the children of God, secure in His hands.

✝ MISSIONAL Application

Record in this space at least one way you will apply the truth of Scripture as one transformed by God and given the new name of Christian by faith in Jesus Christ.

Personal Study 1

Jacob's old name reflects his flawed character.

Read Genesis 32:24-27.

As we will see, Jacob became the namesake for God's chosen people, Israel. Yet the detailed account of Jacob in Genesis reveals a deeply flawed man. He cheated his brother out of his blessing and lied multiple times to his father.

In fact, the author of Genesis provides markers that indicate Jacob's sinful, wandering heart. Genesis often presents traveling east as a bad thing, as a signal that a person was moving away from God (i.e., exile). When Adam and Eve sinned, they were banished to the east, away from God's garden (3:24). After Cain murdered Abel, he went east (4:16). When Lot chose the land near Sodom and Gomorrah, he went east (13:11-12). After Jacob cheated his brother and deceived his father, he traveled toward Paddan-aram and came to the eastern country (29:1).

Still, God kept His promises to Jacob. Remember, the promise included land, offspring, and blessing. God gave Jacob financial blessing (though Jacob schemed to get it), and God blessed him with children. So Jacob had offspring and he had blessing, but what about the land?

This third part of the promise is why the Lord told Jacob to return home to the land promised to his fathers. So Jacob journeyed back toward Canaan as a rich man with a large family; however, another transformation needed to take place—one much more important than family and possessions. As Jacob neared his family's home, he was fearful that his brother, Esau, would seek revenge, so he sent gifts with an envoy ahead of him to soften the blow. As Jacob remained behind, he encountered an unusual "man" who would bring about the greatest change Jacob would experience.

Late in the night, a "man" appeared and began wrestling with Jacob. Later on in the text, it is revealed that this "man" was God Himself. During the wrestling match, the "man" struck Jacob's hip socket and dislocated it.

This wrestling match is instructive in at least two ways. First, the fact that God confronted Jacob hints at the reality of Jacob's flawed character and the truth that God will not allow sin to go unpunished. We see a similar event in the life of Moses when he failed to obey God's command (see Ex. 4:24-26). God wanted to use Jacob, but He wanted to change him first.

Second, the fact that the "man" dislocated Jacob's hip, in what seemed to be a desperate act to get away before sunrise, may point to the reason God held Jacob accountable and wanted to transform him. Before the blessing could be carried forward, Jacob—this sinful deceiver—had to be broken. Perhaps that is why the "man" asked Jacob about his name, which meant "cheater." Jacob's life up to this point had been in line with his name. But now it was time for that to change.

In what ways do our past mistakes sometimes haunt and define us?

How does the gospel help us move beyond those past mistakes?

Personal Study 2

Jacob's new name reflects the grace God has shown him.

Read Genesis 32:28-32.

It is one thing for a person to show grace to someone else. But the effects are multiplied when the God of the universe shows grace to a wretched person. Grace ensures we will never be the same. We see this truth in the life of the cunning deceiver Jacob. Despite Jacob's repeated lying and scheming, God poured out grace upon him, and we see its effect here in Genesis 32.

Even though Jacob was injured in the wrestling match with the "man," he grabbed him and would not let him go. Jacob had already told the "man" his name, which revealed the deceptive nature of his character. But here, in an act of amazing grace, the "man," who happened to be God Himself, allowed Jacob to prevail, and then He renamed him.

Today, we often choose names that are popular at the time or have some family significance to us. But in the ancient world, names indicated someone's character. Names told you about a person's makeup. Therefore, being renamed indicated a change in character—a new start!

Jacob's new name would be "Israel" because he had struggled with God and with men and prevailed (32:28). In a battle of great endurance through a painful injury, Jacob had struggled with God for a blessing and had not given up. Though He would not tell Jacob His name, God blessed him. Then Jacob named the place "Peniel" because he had seen God face to face and been spared (32:30).

Naming the place Peniel indicated that Jacob actually wrestled with God, not a man. Of course, this raises all kinds of theological questions and concerns, such as "How could a man wrestle with God and not be killed instantly?" But the text is not concerned with these matters; rather, its purpose is to show us that Jacob was a transformed man because of his encounter with the gracious Lord. Jacob walked away with a limp, but that was far from the biggest change that night. He limped away a changed man. He did not return to the promised land the same scoundrel that left it years before.

Genesis 32 should encourage us because it reveals that no matter how messed up our lives may be, no matter how many bad decisions we have made, and no matter how much we have wrecked the relationships around us, if we encounter the living God, we can be given a new life. The New Testament teaches that we can encounter God through His Son, Jesus, and that in Christ we bear His name! Therefore, our identity will no longer be wrapped up in our sin, but rather, our identity will be that of beloved children of God.

Not only does Jacob's story teach us about God's gracious patience toward sinners, but it also shows that it often takes a painful encounter with the living God for us to come to our senses. And yet, God's disciplining hand is a sign of His kindness to lead us to repentance and change.

Sometimes we try to change and repair our reputation on our own. How is God's "renaming" us different?

What difficult circumstances has God used to lead you to repentance?

Why were those struggles necessary to lead you to the point of repentance?

Personal Study 3

Jacob's new name reflects the task God has given him.

Read Genesis 35:9-15.

Everyone wants God's blessing. The problem, though, is that many of us do not understand why God blesses His people. We want God to change our lives, but when He does, we don't understand why or for what purpose He has changed us.

In Scripture, we see that God's purpose in blessing His people is not so they will hoard the blessing to themselves. No, God blesses His people so that they will be a blessing to others. We are conduits of blessing. God changes people so that they can be agents of change for others.

God blessed and changed Jacob so he, Israel, would be the means by which God would bring change and blessing to the whole world. In Genesis 35, God reappeared to Jacob and again gave him his new name, which implied the continuing nature of God's promised blessing to Abraham.

Notice the progression for Jacob:

Blessing	New Identity	Responsibility
(v. 9)	*(v. 10)*	*(v. 11)*

In the same way, God blesses us with salvation and transformation so that we can then fulfill His calling on our lives.

At Bethel, God appeared to Jacob again and restated the promises of blessing, land, and offspring. God blessed Jacob and repeated that his new name was Israel. Not only did God bless Jacob, but in an echo of Genesis 1:28, God also commanded Jacob to be fruitful and multiply (35:11). This command would fulfill the promise of offspring. God foretold that a great nation would come from Jacob, and his family line would include kings. Finally, God told Jacob that He would give the land to Jacob and his offspring. Then Jacob set up a stone marker, offered a drink offering, and named the place "Bethel," or "House of God." (This was the same place God made promises to Jacob in Genesis 28.)

God would keep His promises to Jacob. Jacob was indeed fruitful and multiplied. He had twelve sons who would become the twelve tribes of the nation of Israel. And God would keep His promise that through Jacob's offspring would come a King—a Messiah—who would bring salvation to the world.

Significantly, just as God had done with Jacob, his firstborn son would not carry the promise of a king forward. That promise was passed on to Judah (cf. Gen. 49), and through Judah would come the Messiah—Jesus of Nazareth. Jesus would fulfill God's calling on Israel to be a light to the nations, and through His death and resurrection, He would bring salvation to the world.

God had changed Jacob, but He did not do so for Jacob to keep the blessing to himself. Rather, God intended for Jacob's offspring to bring God's saving blessing to the world. The same is true for us. Our salvation does not end with us. God's gracious blessing in our lives through Jesus Christ is intended to move through us as we seek to share the gospel with others and bring salvation to the world.

What are some areas in which we ask for the blessing of God without giving thought to how God might want us to bless others?

How do God's blessings set us up to serve on mission with Him?

God Redeems Joseph's Adversity

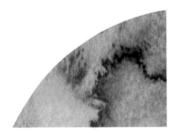
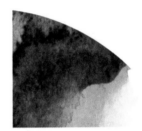
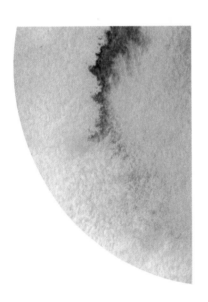

Introducing the Study

Jacob wrestled with God, and he emerged with a limp and a new name. Once a deceiver, Jacob would move forward with the privilege and responsibility of being a part of God's people, tasked to bring God's truth of salvation to the world. Like Jacob, we too have been given a new name—Christians—and we too must move forward by God's grace to live for His glory as trophies of His grace.

What are some ways the Holy Spirit reminded you last week of your new name in Christ?

Sometimes we encounter difficult circumstances that might cause us to question the presence and purpose of God. One of Jacob's sons, Joseph, certainly experienced this kind of adversity. Suffering is challenging, to say the least, but even in our times of pain, we can be sure that God will accomplish His purposes and keep His promises both in and through us to the very end.

 What are some promises of God that can carry us through difficult times?

Setting the Context

Jacob spent the night wrestling with God, and he emerged changed with the new name "**Israel**," a name that would become synonymous with the blessing and ongoing work of God. And then, to his surprise, Jacob was reconciled with his brother, Esau. Jacob then continued on his way to Shechem in the land of Canaan—the land God had chosen for Abraham's descendants to inherit.

✳ How had God proven His faithfulness to Jacob thus far in his life?

Jacob obeyed God's command to return to Bethel, where he built an altar to the Lord, and then he set out toward Bethlehem. But on the way, Jacob's beloved wife, **Rachel**, who was pregnant, began her labor and died during childbirth. Before her death, she delivered one last son for Jacob, **Benjamin**. Jacob was now the father of twelve sons, and the family took up residence where his father, Isaac, had lived.

Jacob did not learn from his parents' mistake of showing favoritism toward their children, and he loved one son more than all the others. **"Joseph's Life"** (p. 83) shows when Jacob gave Joseph, the favored son, a beautiful robe of many colors. So not only was Joseph loved more than his brothers, he now wore his father's favor like a garment, and his older brothers longed to rip it off of him.

How have you seen jealousy cause troubles in families?

✝ CHRIST Connection

God took the evil deeds of Joseph's brothers and used them for His greater plan of providing salvation from the famine. In the same way, God used the evil injustice of those who crucified His Son, Jesus, to bring about His master plan of providing salvation from sin and death.

Joseph's *Life*

In Paddan-aram/Canaan with Family

17 YEARS

- Born, the firstborn son of Jacob's favorite wife, Rachel
- Given a robe of many colors by his father, a symbol of his favored status (age 17)
- Given two dreams picturing him ruling over his family (age 17)
- Thrown in a pit by his brothers and sold to Midianite traders (age 17)

In Slavery/Prison in Egypt

13 YEARS

- Sold as a slave to Potiphar in Egypt (age 17)
- Promoted to Potiphar's personal attendant, in charge of the whole household
- Falsely accused of sexual misconduct by Potiphar's wife and imprisoned
- Given authority over everything under the prison warden
- Became personal attendant to Pharaoh's cupbearer and baker, also in custody (age 28)
- Interpreted dreams of cupbearer and baker, which came true three days later (age 28)

With Authority in Egypt

80 YEARS

- Called before Pharaoh and interpreted his two dreams about a coming famine (age 30)
- Elevated to second-in-command over all of Egypt (age 30)
- Oversaw collection and sale of grain in preparation for and during famine (age 30-44)

71 Years with Family in Egypt

- Reconciled with brothers; reunited with father and family (age 39)
- Died and buried in Egypt, but with hope of returning to promised land (age 110)

Continuing the Discussion

 Watch this session's video, and then continue the group discussion using the following guide.

How did God show Himself faithful to His promises throughout the adversity in Joseph's life?

How does the story of Joseph give you confidence to endure hardship and continue on in faith?

As a group, read Genesis 37:5-8,18-20,23-28.

 What do you think Joseph was thinking or praying as he was betrayed by his brothers?

How do you see God's work even through this betrayal?

The favoritism that Jacob extended to Joseph caused a rift between Joseph and his brothers. This combined with the way Joseph shared his dreams with his brothers resulted in Joseph's brothers being so consumed with anger that they threw him in a pit, sold him into slavery, and let Jacob think that Joseph had been killed by a wild animal. But God's work was not hindered in the betrayal, for God was beginning to position Joseph to play a significant role in His redemptive plan.

As a group, read Genesis 39:19-23.

 How do you think Joseph kept from getting bitter during these events?

Can you share some ways you have been reminded of God's presence even during affliction?

Joseph's life reads like an elevator, with constant ups and downs. He showed his integrity in the house of Potiphar only to be imprisoned. His faith in the continuing promises and work of God was the only way not to become bitter at these twists and turns in life.

As a group, read Genesis 50:15-21.

> What does Joseph's response to his brothers reveal about his faith?

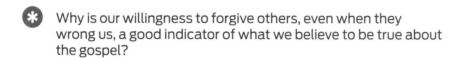 Why is our willingness to forgive others, even when they wrong us, a good indicator of what we believe to be true about the gospel?

Though his brothers clearly wronged him, Joseph acknowledged the continuing ability and willingness of God to take evil and injustice and work it for good. The ultimate example of this is the cross, as God used the evil of those who crucified His Son to bring about His master plan of providing salvation from sin and death.

✝ MISSIONAL Application

Record in this space at least one way you will apply the truth of Scripture as a sinner whom God has forgiven completely through faith in Jesus Christ.

Personal Study 1

God is working even through Joseph's betrayal.

Read Genesis 37:5-8,18-20,23-28.

We've seen how God made gracious covenant promises to Abraham, Isaac, and Jacob. But God also warned Abraham about a future slavery in a foreign land before they would receive the promised land (Gen. 15:13). So yes, God's plan was to bless the entire world through Abraham's offspring, but that future plan included pain and suffering.

That's where the story of Joseph (one of Jacob's sons) comes in. In Genesis 37, we see God reveal His plan for Joseph's future.

Joseph was Jacob's favorite son because he was born to Jacob's favorite wife, Rachel (Gen. 30:22-24). That's why Jacob made Joseph a robe of many colors, a sign of Joseph's favored status and an outlet of anger for Joseph's brothers, who despised him.

Making matters worse, Joseph had two dreams about his brothers bowing down to him—not something you want to hear from your younger brother. The text doesn't indicate if Joseph was right or wrong in recounting these dreams to his family, but it's clear that the dreams were a picture of God's future plan.

These dreams seemed to serve as the last straw for Joseph's brothers, and they betrayed their younger brother and sold him into slavery. Surely few pains run deeper than betrayal, especially by those you should be able to trust. No matter their reason for being so angry and jealous of Joseph, the brothers sinned, and the consequences could not be undone.

From a human perspective, we might look at such a betrayal as evidence of God's absence. Where was God? Why didn't He stop such a terrible action? But the story of Joseph's betrayal reminds us of the incredible ability of God to bring good from evil. God promises that all things—including something as sinful as this betrayal—will eventually work out for both the good of the believer and the glory of God. Like a master artist weaving together a tapestry, God is able to take the sinful decisions of humankind and frustrate their evil intent as He continues to work out His plan.

Though Joseph's betrayal was great, it was only a shadow of what God's own Son, Jesus, would later experience. He too was betrayed, not to slavery but to death. He was crucified by the very people He came to save. But even this most sinful of acts played a role in God's overall plan, for just as God was working through Joseph's betrayal to bring good, so also would He work through the betrayal of Jesus, using the evil injustice of those who crucified Him to bring salvation.

Because of this, we can be confident today when we experience betrayal and other wrongs. We can know that no matter how much we may not like what God is doing, we can trust that God's plan for our future is better than any plan we could come up with for ourselves. Pain in God's hand is better than comfort apart from it. We can trust His plan for the future even when we do not like or understand our present circumstances.

When you read the text, do you get the sense that Joseph was justified in telling his family about his dreams? Or do you see him as proud and arrogant? Why?

How might we envy God's plan for someone else's life rather than accept the one He has laid out for us?

Personal Study 2

God is present even through Joseph's affliction.

Read Genesis 39:19-23.

Although Joseph was betrayed by his brothers and sold into slavery in Egypt apart from his family, God was with him. Joseph became a servant in the house of Potiphar, one of Pharaoh's officers and the captain of the guards. Because God was with Joseph and prospered everything that he did, Potiphar put Joseph in charge of his entire house, and the Lord blessed Potiphar's house greatly. This shows an example of how God continued to keep His promise to Abraham that He would bless everyone who blessed Abraham (Gen. 12:3).

But just as things were looking up, they went from bad to worse. The eye of Potiphar's wife fell on Joseph, and she began to proposition him day after day to sleep with her, but Joseph refused each time. She continued her advances until one day she grabbed him by his clothing. Joseph fled, leaving his garment behind, and that gave Potiphar's spurned wife evidence to make a false accusation against Joseph.

Joseph did the right thing in rejecting the sexual advances of his master's wife. Even so, he was falsely accused, and despite his innocence, he was thrown into prison. Yet even there, the Lord was with him (39:21). He was not alone. God had not abandoned him. God gave Joseph great grace so that even the prison warden put Joseph in charge of all the other prisoners. And once again, the Lord prospered everything that Joseph did.

Too many Christians have the false idea that if God is with us, then nothing bad will happen. We think of verses like Romans 8:31—"If God is for us, who is against us?"—as if they promise life without adversity, but we leave out the verses that say it is likely we will experience suffering, famine, nakedness, peril, and many other obstacles (8:35-39). Rightly understood, nothing can separate you from God and His love in Christ, not because He shields you from bad things but rather because in the midst of those circumstances, He walks with you. He brings you safely through to the other side.

We are tempted in tough moments to question if God is with us, but the Bible assures us that He never leaves nor forsakes His people (Deut. 31:6; Heb. 13:5). Our hope is not in a God who keeps bad things from happening to us. Our hope is in a God who is with us in life and death, a God who sees to it that nothing separates us from His love in Jesus Christ, and a God who can and will use even bad things for good.

Joseph's life points forward to Jesus. Jesus would be betrayed, handed over to captivity, stripped of His robe, unjustly sentenced, and killed. But the rejection and humiliation of Jesus was at the center of God's plan to save Israel and the world! Jesus looked abandoned by God, as if His cries to the Father went unanswered, but when that grave opened on Sunday morning, it was clear He was not alone. God vindicated His Son.

We get a glimpse of this plan in Joseph's life. He suffered. It seemed as if he were abandoned, but God was with him and God was accomplishing His good plan. Joseph was a righteous sufferer, and God was with him. He succeeded in captivity, and his humiliation eventually led to his exaltation to bless Israel and other nations (cf. Gen. 12; Phil. 2).

What lessons can we learn from Joseph's victory over temptation?

What are some instances in your life when it seemed like God was absent? What are some instances when you clearly felt His presence?

How does the knowledge that God is with you in hardship help you battle things like discouragement, anxiety, and isolation?

Personal Study 3

God is faithful even to overrule evil with good.

Read Genesis 50:15-21.

You've probably heard the proverb "Two wrongs don't make a right." Just because someone mistreats you does not give you the right to mistreat that person. Repaying evil with evil may be our sinful urge and the way of the world, but it is not the way God works—nor the way God's people should work.

As we pick back up with the story of Joseph, we see that Israel took his family down to Egypt to live there during the famine. At the time, they numbered around seventy people (Gen. 46:27). But God blessed them in Egypt and made them rich, and they multiplied (47:27).

Remember, God had promised to bless the whole world through Abraham's offspring. So before he died, Jacob restated these promises from God to his sons and foretold that the Messiah would come from Judah (49:8-10). When Jacob died, Joseph and his brothers took their father's body to the promised land for burial. When they returned to Egypt, Joseph's brothers were concerned that he would get his revenge now that their father was dead. Perhaps Joseph had just restrained his anger out of consideration for their father.

So, the brothers sent word to Joseph that before their father's death, he told them that he wanted Joseph to forgive everything his brothers did to him. Joseph cried when he heard this. His brothers bowed before him and told him they would serve him.

But Joseph told them not to be afraid, and he indicated that he trusted in God's justice. He told them he knew he was where God wanted him to be—what they intended for evil, God used for good to save many lives. Although the journey was difficult and Joseph suffered greatly, God used it to bring him where he was so he could save their family from the famine. So Joseph forgave his brothers, comforted them, and took care of them and their families. He showed amazing grace to his brothers.

Joseph went on to live a long life. When he died, he was placed in a temporary tomb in Egypt, his remains waiting to return with God's people to the promised land. Genesis begins with life in paradise, but it ends with death in a temporary tomb outside the promised land. God made a covenant with Abraham, but the promises were still unfulfilled. But the story is not over...

Joseph's life was a preview of the coming Messiah who would forgive those who wronged Him. Joseph knew that God used his brothers' sinful actions to save many people. Jesus would be mistreated, betrayed for silver, handed over to captivity, and ultimately executed at the hands of evil men. While He was being crucified, He looked upon those killing Him with a forgiving heart (see Luke 23:34). On the cross, He secured saving forgiveness for the world, and then God highly exalted Him so that the nations of the world would stream to Him, bow the knee, and confess Him as Lord (Phil. 2:5-11; cf. Isa. 45:22-23). Evil men killed the Messiah, but God used even their evil deeds to accomplish His goal of salvation.

What wrong actions toward you would make you consider someone an "enemy"?

How can we show our enemies love and mercy as an expression of God's love for us?

How does the gospel help you put the bad things that happen in your life in the right perspective?

Tips for Leading a Small Group

Follow these guidelines to prepare for each group session.

Prayerfully Prepare

Review
Review the weekly material and group questions ahead of time.

Pray
Be intentional about praying for each person in the group. Ask the Holy Spirit to work through you and the group discussion as you point to Jesus each week through God's Word.

Minimize Distractions

Create a comfortable environment. If group members are uncomfortable, they'll be distracted and therefore not engaged in the group experience. Plan ahead by considering these details:

Seating

Temperature

Lighting

Food or Drink

Surrounding Noise

General Cleanliness

At best, thoughtfulness and hospitality show guests and group members they're welcome and valued in whatever environment you choose to gather. At worst, people may never notice your effort, but they're also not distracted. Do everything in your ability to help people focus on what's most important: connecting with God, with the Bible, and with one another.

Include Others

Your goal is to foster a community in which people are welcome just as they are but encouraged to grow spiritually. Always be aware of opportunities to include any people who visit the group and to invite new people to join your group. An inexpensive way to make first-time guests feel welcome or to invite someone to get involved is to give them their own copies of this Bible study book.

Encourage Discussion

A good small-group experience has the following characteristics.

Everyone Participates
Encourage everyone to ask questions, share responses, or read aloud.

No One Dominates—Not Even the Leader
Be sure that your time speaking as a leader takes up less than half of your time together as a group. Politely guide discussion if anyone dominates.

Nobody Is Rushed Through Questions
Don't feel that a moment of silence is a bad thing. People often need time to think about their responses to questions they've just heard or to gain courage to share what God is stirring in their hearts.

Input Is Affirmed and Followed Up
Make sure you point out something true or helpful in a response. Don't just move on. Build community with follow-up questions, asking how other people have experienced similar things or how a truth has shaped their understanding of God and the Scripture you're studying. People are less likely to speak up if they fear that you don't actually want to hear their answers or that you're looking for only a certain answer.

God and His Word Are Central
Opinions and experiences can be helpful, but God has given us the truth. Trust God's Word to be the authority and God's Spirit to work in people's lives. You can't change anyone, but God can. Continually point people to the Word and to active steps of faith.

How to Use the Leader Guide

Prepare to Lead

Each session of the Leader Guide is designed to be **torn out** so you, the leader, can have this front-and-back page with you as you lead your group through the session.

Watch the session teaching video and **read through the session content** with the Leader Guide tear-out in hand and notice how it supplements each section of the study.

Use the **Session Objective** in the Leader Guide to help focus your preparation and leadership in the group session.

Questions and Answers

✳ Questions in the session content with **this icon** have some sample answers provided in the Leader Guide, if needed, to help you jump-start the conversation or steer the conversation.

Setting the Context

This section of the session always has an **infographic** on the opposite page. The Leader Guide provides an activity to help your group members interact with the content communicated through the infographic.

MISSIONAL Application

The Leader Guide provides a **MISSIONAL Application statement** about how Christians should respond to the truth of God's Word. Read this statement to the group and then direct them to record in the blank space provided in their book at least one way they will respond on a personal level, remembering that all of Scripture points to the gospel of Jesus Christ.

Pray

Conclude each group session with a prayer. **A brief sample prayer** is provided at the end of each Leader Guide tear-out.

Session 1 · Leader Guide

Session Objective

Show God's good purpose in creation, specifically how He positioned humankind to bear His image and glorify Him through our ruling over creation, our relationships with Him and one another, and our work and service for Him.

Introducing the Study

Use these answers as needed for the questions highlighted in this section.

- All that we experience as a part of creation had a beginning, so it is not ultimate in our lives.
- God, who was before all things, is the greatest reality ever to exist, and all of our reality must be interpreted through Him.

- In Genesis 1:1, we meet a God who is simply there. The Bible is God's revelation of Himself, not an argument for His existence.
- God existed before the beginning; therefore, He is outside of time and is eternal.
- We see that God is present and active in His creation from the very beginning.

Read this paragraph to transition to the next part of the study.

God is the One who created everything we see and know. It is from Him that we understand the meaning of our own lives. It is through Him that all things continue to hold together in our world today. And it is to Him that all glory is properly due.

Setting the Context

Use the following activity to help group members see the significance of a Christ-centered reading of Scripture.

Ask group members to look at **"Seeing Jesus in Genesis"** (p. 11) and to come up with a statement that ties together and summarizes these five Old and New Testament connections from the Book of Genesis. *(Example: Jesus sets right what humanity destroys through their sin, and He does so by sacrificing Himself for the sake of humanity.)*

A good summary statement here will lay the foundation for the gospel of Jesus, who died on the cross for the sin of the world. If the basics of the gospel can be found foreshadowed in the first book of the Bible, then imagine how much the rest of Scripture points to the Son, the Word of God, who created all things with the plan and purpose to lay His life down for God's image bearers.

Continuing the Discussion

Watch this session's video, and then as part of the group discussion, use these answers as needed for the questions highlighted in this section.

Genesis 1:1-2,31

- God is eternal and exists outside of time.
- God is all-powerful, the Creator of all things.
- God is good.

Genesis 1:26-28; 2:16-25

- Recognizing the image of God in other people will help us to treat them with respect and dignity, whether they are as yet unborn, among the elderly, an acquaintance, an unknown, or counted as family, friend, or foe.
- Seeing people as created in the image of God, just as we are, can help us spot injustice in the world and work toward justice for the oppressed.
- Treating people with respect as image bearers of God honors the God who made all human beings.

Colossians 1:15-17

- We can no longer take things for granted nor live for our own selfish pursuits and desires.
- Everything we see and interact with and use in creation should serve the purpose of honoring the Son of God.
- People who live only to please themselves are missing their true purpose in life, and we who know Christ can share His gospel with them.

Share the following statement with the group. Then direct them to record in the space provided in their book at least one way they will apply the truth of Scripture as an image bearer of God.

MISSIONAL Application

Because we are image bearers of our good Creator God, reflect His glory in how you steward the earth, work and rest, and cultivate relationships with Him and others in the name of Jesus Christ.

Close your group in prayer, thanking God for His creative power and praying for a greater vision to live out what it means to bear His image.

Session 2 · Leader Guide

Session Objective

Show how deep and widespread sin is by surveying the rapid descent in Genesis 3–11. The main takeaway should be how terrible our sin is and how God is right to judge us for it, but still we see God's hope and grace all along the way.

Introducing the Study

Use these answers as needed for the question highlighted in this section.

- We begin to live only for ourselves, satisfying our selfish desires with no thought of Creator God or anyone else, for that matter.
- We start taking the blessings and benefits of creation for granted, believing we are owed as the center of our universe.
- We begin working and tiring out as though the weight of sustaining the universe were on our shoulders.

Setting the Context

Use these answers as needed for the question highlighted in this section.

- God has perfect relationship within Himself as Father, Son, and Spirit, so our creation was not a necessity but an overflow of God's perfect love.
- Being made in the image of the triune God means we were created as relational beings. We were not meant to live our lives alone and distant from others.
- God created human beings to be blessed by having a relationship with Him.

Use the following activity to help group members see the grace of God in providing salvation for sinners who likewise deserve judgment along with the wicked.

On a scale of 1 to 10 (1 being carefree; 10 being holy wrath), ask group members to plot their own sense of justice and judgment when they have been wronged and sinned against by someone else. Then ask group members to look at **"Salvation Through Judgment"** (p. 23) and to reflect specifically on *the means* of God's judgment (a "10") in comparison with our own sense of judgment. Then encourage them to see God's amazing grace in the *salvation* column to save sinners who deserve His judgment.

Read this paragraph to transition to the next part of the study.

While the theme of sinfulness is pervasive in Genesis 3–11, so also is the refrain of God's love and grace. Keep an eye out for the signs of God's "salvation through judgment" as we continue our discussion.

Continuing the Discussion

Watch this session's video, and then as part of the group discussion, use these answers as needed for the questions highlighted in this section.

Genesis 3:1-7

- Acts of sin in our own lives show a distrust of God and His Word.
- Sin is appealing to our eyes and our desires, and we can easily rationalize our choices to give in to sin.
- Sin always results in shame and broken relationships.

Genesis 6:5-8

- We should want to live holy lives in the fear of the Lord.
- We should recognize and be grateful for the grace God has shown to us in Jesus Christ taking upon Himself the judgment for our sins.
- We should care for the sinners who remain under God's judgment, and we should share with them the reality of God's judgment and the good news of the Savior who came to rescue us.

Genesis 11:1-9

- Sin rejects the wisdom and authority of Creator God, who made us and everything around us.
- Sin is choosing to go my own way instead of God's way, essentially making myself the god of my own life.
- Sin takes advantage of people, putting one's own interests above the interests of others, so that we see people beneath us and ourselves as supreme.

Share the following statement with the group. Then direct them to record in the space provided in their book at least one way they will apply the truth of Scripture as a sinner who knows of the grace of God in Jesus Christ.

✝ MISSIONAL Application

Because we are recipients of God's grace through Jesus, we proclaim the reality of God's righteousness and grace to others so they may join His family and be saved from the coming judgment of sin.

Close your group in prayer, asking God for wisdom to identify sin for what it truly is and to help others do the same so we can find grace and forgiveness in Jesus.

Session 3 · Leader Guide

Session Objective

Show how God formed a new people through Abraham and how God would use this people to bring the answer for sin—Jesus, who provides salvation for all who have faith in Him.

Introducing the Study

Use these answers as needed for the question highlighted in this section.

- So we can be encouraged toward humility, recognizing that God's global mission included reaching us.
- That we would resist cultural pride and refrain from seeing ourselves and our culture as better or more deserving than others.
- So we can participate in the spread of the gospel around the world, through our going, giving, and sending.

Setting the Context

Use these answers as needed for the question highlighted in this section.

- Isolation and suspicion
- Misunderstanding, frustration, and anger
- Racial discord, competition, and feelings of superiority

Use the following activity to help group members grasp the reality and implications of faith in God to fulfill His promises.

On **"Abram's Journey"** (p. 35), point out Ur at the starting point of Abram's migration, and note the location of Babylon on the route to Haran and then Canaan, the promised land. Ask someone to estimate the distance traveled from Ur to Canaan *(about 1,200 miles)*, and then ask the group how far such a distance would take them from your present location. Invite them to imagine leaving their home and extended family to move there based solely on the promises of God. Then ask the following questions: What challenges and difficulties might you encounter? What would faith in God's promises require of you?

Read this paragraph to transition to the next part of the study.

Abram obeyed God's call to leave his home and family and travel to an unknown land, all in faith that God would do what He said He would do. Abram had his share of doubt and missteps on his journey, but God kept showing up, and Abram believed.

Continuing the Discussion

Watch this session's video, and then as part of the group discussion, use these answers as needed for the questions highlighted in this section.

Genesis 12:1-4

- By necessity, faith leads to obedience.
- Faith is not based on evidence of a promise's fulfillment but based on the goodness and reliability of the One who makes the promise.
- Faith in God will lead to choices that defy the expectations of the world.

Genesis 15:1-6

- We might try to secretly network with people to ensure our own security at work or achieve a desired outcome, even at the expense of another's well-being.
- We can act on our own without prayer or wisdom from God's Word and from God's people.
- We might seek vengeance against someone who has offended us, even though God says vengeance is His to repay (Rom. 12:19).

Genesis 17:1-10

- God calls Christians to love others unconditionally, regardless of family, culture, socio-economic status, or race.
- Christians should live holy lives reflecting the goodness of God and His wisdom for relating to others and creation.
- Christians are called to live for the mission of God and His glory rather than for their own personal kingdoms on this earth.

Share the following statement with the group. Then direct them to record in the space provided in their book at least one way they will apply the truth of Scripture as one who recognizes that God credits righteousness to those who believe in His Son, Jesus Christ.

✝ MISSIONAL Application

Because we have been made part of Abraham's family of faith through Christ, we live as people through whom God's blessings may flow to the world.

Close your group in prayer, asking God to help you and your group live holy lives amongst the peoples and nations of the world, set apart for the glory of God in Christ.

Session 4 · Leader Guide

Session Objective
Show how God tested Abraham to reveal his faith in God's promise to bring salvation to the world through his family, and also explain the types of Jesus we see in Isaac on the altar and the substitute ram.

Introducing the Study
Use these answers as needed for the questions highlighted in this section.

- Since we are Abraham's children by faith in Jesus (Rom. 4:16), we should be looking for ways to bless the world in the name of Jesus.
- We should be active in trying to pass on the faith to our family members, friends, and coworkers.
- We should live with an attitude of gratitude for being included by faith in the blessing given to Abraham's descendants.

- Faith ought to grow in a person rather than remain stagnant, and testing is a means God uses to grow our faith.
- Abraham's circumstances had changed drastically over the years, and testing his faith would reveal to Abraham where he was placing his trust.
- Faith is demonstrated and perfected in ongoing obedience (Jas. 2:22-23).

Setting the Context
Use the following activity to help group members see how the Lord provides both preparation for tests and in the midst of tests.

Instruct group members to look at the first row on **"The LORD Will Provide"** (p. 47). Then ask the following questions:

- "How does the phrase 'only son' recall God's preparation of Abraham leading up to the test He was about to give him?" *(God had promised a son to Abraham and Sarah, and though they had taken matters into their own hands on more than one occasion, the Lord preserved them and His promise. And He fulfilled His promise through a miracle in their old age. The Lord had been faithful to His word, and He wouldn't change that with this test.)*

- "How do the next three rows relate to the first?" *(The Israelites were the people descended from Abraham through Isaac. The Lord provided atonement for their sins through sacrifices. But Jesus, Abraham's promised "seed," was the ultimate sacrifice for sin, and in Him is the blessing to all peoples that the Lord promised through Abraham.)*

Continuing the Discussion

Watch this session's video, and then as part of the group discussion, use these answers as needed for the questions highlighted in this section.

Genesis 22:1-6

- Believing God is good and faithful even when circumstances challenge that belief.
- Faith means laying down everything we want or have in order to obey God.
- Believing God can do the impossible and that He will keep His word.

Genesis 22:7-14

- Abraham had received in his old age a son to carry on his legacy, and here he was willing to sacrifice his son because God had told him to.
- Abraham trusted God completely for the well-being of himself, his son, and the entire world.
- Abraham's willingness to obey gave evidence of his faith in God and set the example of faith in God/Jesus for all who would come after him.

Hebrews 11:17-19

- Christians must believe in the resurrection of Jesus or else we are without hope and remain dead in our sins.
- Christians believe that God has a blessing for the entire world in Jesus, so we must tell about how the Lord has provided Jesus for our salvation from sin.
- We can faithfully share the gospel without fear of consequences because we believe and know that God has the power to raise the dead.

Share the following statement with the group. Then direct them to record in the space provided in their book at least one way they will apply the truth of Scripture as one who believes in the resurrection power of the Lord, both physically and spiritually.

MISSIONAL Application

Because we are people who have realized the fullness of God's promise and been saved by God's sacrifice of His Son, we trust God with full confidence in His resurrection power, willing to sacrifice all for His mission.

Close your group in prayer, asking God to help you and your group live as those who are confident in the resurrection from the dead.

Session 5 · Leader Guide

Session Objective

Show how God used a dysfunctional family plagued with sin and strife to bring about His purposes, revealing that the success of God's plan is not based on our merit but on His power, mercy, and grace.

Introducing the Study

Use these answers as needed for the question highlighted in this section.

- There are no "likely people" to use, for there is no one good (Rom. 3:10).
- When God uses unlikely people, it brings the glory to Him and Him alone.
- God's using unlikely people highlights His power, mercy, and grace.

Read this sentence to transition to the next part of the study.

Sin could not stop God's plan, rather God moved His plan to deal with the sin of the world forward not by working around sinful humanity but through them.

Setting the Context

Use these answers as needed for the question highlighted in this section.

- God had made promises and kept them, so Abraham had every reason to think God would keep on keeping His promises.
- God's promises were not fulfilled in the ways he expected, so he had to trust God even when things were beyond his own understanding.
- God had been faithful to him in spite of his unfaithfulness, so God's promises were sure.

Use the following activity to help group members see the depth of God's power, mercy, and grace.

Call attention to **"The Patriarchs"** (p. 59), and recount the following facts about the patriarchs. **Abraham:** Believed God's promises; twice lied about Sarah being his sister; tried to build his family through Sarah's servant; laughed at the thought of God giving a son to him and Sarah in their old age. **Isaac:** Prayed for Rebekah to have children; lied about Rebekah being his sister; showed favoritism between his sons; ignored God's word about the older serving the younger. **Jacob:** Lied and deceived his family members; showed favoritism between his sons; believed God's promises.

Ask: "At what point would you have given up on this family and started over?" Then state: "God's ways are higher than our ways (Isa. 55:8-9); our salvation is proof of that."

Continuing the Discussion

Watch this session's video, and then as part of the group discussion, use these answers as needed for the questions highlighted in this section.

Genesis 27:1-10

- Human beings are to submit in faith to God's plan and purpose for the world and everything in it.
- Human beings should obey the revealed will of God in Scripture—love God and love others.
- Human beings should not take matters into their own hands for their own purposes.

Genesis 27:18-20,25-29

- Human beings are by nature selfish and self-centered.
- We fear consequences but can easily justify our actions to gain what we want.
- We are prone to use anyone, even the people we love, to fulfill our desires.

Genesis 28:10-15

- No, Jacob did not deserve God's blessing. This reveals God's great faithfulness to His promises—He will do what He said He will do.
- God is a God of grace and mercy, and He will never cast out His children.
- Relationship with God is ultimately not a matter of what we do but what He has done.

Share the following statement with the group. Then direct them to record in the space provided in their book at least one way they will apply the truth of Scripture as an unworthy sinner who has received the grace and mercy of God through faith in Jesus Christ.

MISSIONAL Application

Because God has shown mercy to us, an unworthy people, we look for ways God can demonstrate His mercy and grace to others through our struggles, flaws, and dysfunctions.

Close your group in prayer, thanking God that His blessing of the gospel is not dependent on our goodness but on His grace.

Session 6 · Leader Guide

Session Objective

Show that even while God can work through His people no matter what, in His kindness, God works in us to change us for our good and His glory.

Introducing the Study

Use these answers as needed for the questions highlighted in this section.

- The gospel was freely shared with us, so we should freely share it with others.
- God's mercy to me, an undeserving sinner, leads me to praise God, and I want others to know what He has done for me and can do for them.

- We must remember that our growth in the faith comes from what Jesus has done for us.
- Our sanctification is part of our salvation, and we can do neither on our own.
- Continually reflecting on the gospel will help us resist pride and desire to share the gospel with others.

Setting the Context

Use the following activity to help group members see God's plan of redemption at work.

Ask group members to look at **"Jacob's Family"** (p. 71) and number the sons of Jacob *(answer: twelve)*. Point out that God changes Jacob's name to "Israel," so the children of Jacob become the twelve tribes of Israel, but still not in the way we would expect.

- **Levi:** The Levites become the tribe of priests and are not considered one of the twelve tribes of Israel because they belong to the Lord.

- **Joseph:** This son is favored by Jacob, being the first son of his beloved wife, Rachel. He himself is not considered one of the twelve tribes but instead gets a double portion of Jacob's inheritance because his two sons are taken by Jacob and blessed as sons equal with their uncles.

- **Judah:** The promised line of kings that God had declared would come through Abraham, Isaac, and Jacob comes not through Jacob's firstborn son, Reuben, nor through his favored son, Joseph, but through his fourth son. And the promise is carried on through Perez on account of some more sinful activity in Genesis 38. Judah is front and center in the struggles in Joseph's life, but God works in him to change him, just as He works in Jacob's life.

Continuing the Discussion

Watch this session's video, and then as part of the group discussion, use these answers as needed for the questions highlighted in this section.

Genesis 32:24-27

- God is merciful toward His children.
- God is gentle and patient with His children.
- God asks questions with a purpose.

Genesis 32:28-32

- Jacob's old name described who he was—a deceiver.
- God changes people so we are no longer who we were but who God wants us to be.
- Jacob's character needed work, and God accomplishes that work Himself.

Genesis 35:9-15

- When we are tempted to sin.
- When we have sinned.
- When we struggle with doubts and depression in the midst of our circumstances.

Share the following statement with the group. Then direct them to record in the space provided in their book at least one way they will apply the truth of Scripture as one transformed by God and given the new name of Christian by faith in Jesus Christ.

✝ MISSIONAL Application

Because we have been given the new name of Christians, we strive to live in a manner worthy of our new name so that others may praise God for His transforming power.

Close your group in prayer, asking God to remind you this week of your new name in Christ.

Session 7 · Leader Guide

Session Objective

Show how God will bring about His plan not only through sinful people, as we saw with Jacob's family, but also through sinful situations—nothing will prevent the fulfillment of His promise.

Introducing the Study

Use these answers as needed for the question highlighted in this section.

- God said, "I will never leave you or abandon you" (Heb. 13:5; Deut. 31:6,8).
- "He who started a good work in you will carry it on to completion until the day of Christ Jesus" (Phil. 1:6).
- "Neither death nor life, nor angels nor rulers, nor things present nor things to come, nor powers, nor height nor depth, nor any other created thing will be able to separate us from the love of God that is in Christ Jesus our Lord" (Rom. 8:38-39).
- "You will have suffering in this world. Be courageous! I have conquered the world" (John 16:33).

Setting the Context

Use these answers as needed for the question highlighted in this section.

- The Lord had watched over Jacob as He promised and brought him back to the land promised to his fathers (Gen. 28:15).
- Jacob had numerous offspring, a fulfillment of God's promises to Abraham, Isaac, and himself.
- God was changing the heart and character of this deceiver into one who trusted in the Lord for his welfare and provision.

Use the following activity to help group members see how the life of Joseph points forward to the life, death, and resurrection of Jesus.

Ask group members to look over the summary of **"Joseph's Life"** (p. 83) and to note connections and parallels with Jesus' life, death, and resurrection. *(The pattern of Joseph's life is one of favor, humiliation, and then exaltation, just like the pattern of Jesus' preexistence, incarnation, crucifixion, resurrection, and ascension. Furthermore, Jesus is betrayed, oppressed, falsely accused, and lifted up to be the blessing to the world, in which He reconciles people from every tribe, tongue, and nation together as one family of God through faith in Him.)*

Continuing the Discussion

Watch this session's video, and then as part of the group discussion, use these answers as needed for the questions highlighted in this section.

Genesis 37:5-8,18-20,23-28

- He could have been thinking about justice, revenge, and vengeance.
- He might have prayed to God with questions and doubts because his circumstances were nothing like his dreams.
- He likely prayed to be rescued and returned to his father and family.

Genesis 39:19-23

- He recognized that the Lord was with him and hadn't forsaken him.
- He continued on with what he knew to do: obey the Lord and be a blessing to others.
- He looked for the blessings of God even in the midst of his unjust suffering and hardship.

Genesis 50:15-21

- When we recognize the depth of God's mercy and grace to forgive us as unworthy sinners, we can have a heart filled with God's grace and mercy to forgive others.
- The gospel says that no one is beyond the reach of God's forgiveness, so we shouldn't withhold our forgiveness either, as if we were higher than God.
- Jesus came into the world to save sinners, and He forgave the sinners who crucified Him; we can do no less than forgive as our Savior did.

Share the following statement with the group. Then direct them to record in the space provided in their book at least one way they will apply the truth of Scripture as a sinner whom God has forgiven completely through faith in Jesus Christ.

MISSIONAL Application

Because we are a forgiven people through Christ, we forgive those who sin against us, recognizing that God is working everything to the good of those who love Him.

Close your group in prayer, praying specifically for those in your group to remain faithful during seasons of adversity.

**BE DILIGENT
TO PRESENT
YOURSELF TO GOD
AS ONE APPROVED,**
a worker who
doesn't need
to be ashamed,
correctly teaching
the word of truth.
2 TIMOTHY 2:15

FROM COVER
TO COVER,

the Bible is the story of God's plan to redeem sinners through Jesus—the gospel. Gospel Foundations tells that story.

——————

Be sure to take advantage of the following resources if you're planning a churchwide study. Even the *Single Group Starter Pack* offers significant savings.

CHURCH LAUNCH KIT (DIGITAL)

Want to take your entire church through Gospel Foundations? You'll want a *Church Launch Kit*. It includes sermon outlines, promotional graphics, and a Wordsearch Bible digital library for all leaders valued at $330. The *Kit* comes complimentary with every *Church Starter Pack*. Also available separately.

$29.99

——

Order online, call 800.458.2772, or visit the LifeWay Christian Store serving you.

STARTER PACKS

You can save money and time by purchasing starter packs for your group or church. Every *Church Starter Pack* includes a digital *Church Launch Kit* and access to a digital version of the *Leader Kit* videos.

Single Group Starter Pack
(10 *Bible Study Books*, 1 *Leader Kit*)
$99.99

Church Starter Pack - Small
(50 *Bible Study Books*, 5 *Leader Kit* DVDs, *Church Launch Kit*)
$449.99

Church Starter Pack - Medium
(100 *Bible Study Books*, 10 *Leader Kit* DVDs, *Church Launch Kit*)
$799.99

Church Starter Pack - Large
(500 *Bible Study Books*, 50 *Leader Kit* DVDs, *Church Launch Kit*)
$3495.99

LifeWay.com/GospelFoundations

Prices and availability subject to change without notice.